SINGING FROM THE HEART

*Discovering Worship
That Rejoices
and Restores*

A Study of the Psalms

Jack W. Hayford
with
Joseph Snider

THOMAS NELSON PUBLISHERS
Nashville

CONTENTS

About the General Editor/About the Writer 4

The Gift That Keeps on Giving 5

Lesson 1:   A Song of Wisdom.. 10

Lesson 2:   A Song of Creation 23

Lesson 3:   A Song of Joy 35

Lesson 4:   A Song of Sorrow 48

Lesson 5:   A Song of Trust 60

Lesson 6:   A Song of Fear... 72

Lesson 7:   A Song of Protection 83

Lesson 8:   A Song of Thanksgiving...................................... 95

Lesson 9:   A Song of God's Word.......................................107

Lesson 10: A Song of the Messiah 115

Lesson 11: A Song of Repentance.......................................128

Lesson 12: A Song of Salvation...138

Lesson 13: A Song of Witness...149

Singing from the Heart: Discovering Worship That Rejoices and Restores (A Study of the Psalms) is one of a series of study guides that focus exciting, discovery-geared coverage of Bible book and power themes—all prompting toward dynamic, Holy Spirit-filled living.

About the General Editor

JACK W. HAYFORD, noted pastor, teacher, writer, and composer, is the General Editor of the complete series, working with the publisher in the conceiving and developing of each of the books.

Dr. Hayford is Senior Pastor of The Church On The Way, the First Foursquare Church of Van Nuys, California. He and his wife, Anna, have four married children, all of whom are active in either pastoral ministry or vital church life. As General Editor of the *Spirit-Filled Life Bible*, Pastor Hayford led a four-year project, which has resulted in the availability of one of today's most practical and popular study Bibles. He is author of more than twenty books, including *A Passion for Fullness, The Beauty of Spiritual Language, Rebuilding the Real You,* and *Prayer Is Invading the Impossible.* His musical compositions number over four hundred songs, including the widely sung "Majesty."

About the Writer

JOSEPH SNIDER has worked in Christian ministry for twenty-two years. In addition to freelance writing and speaking, he worked three years with Young Life, served for seven years on the Christian Education faculty at Fort Wayne Bible College, and pastored churches in Indianapolis and Fort Wayne, Indiana. He currently enjoys part-time teaching at Franklin College in Franklin, Indiana. His writing includes material for Thomas Nelson Publishers, Moody Magazine, Union Gospel Press, and David C. Cook.

Married to Sally Snider, Joe has two children: Jenny is 21 and Ted is 18. They live in Indianapolis, Indiana. Joe earned a B.A. in English from Cedarville College in Cedarville, Ohio, and a Th.M. in Christian Education from Dallas Theological Seminary.

Of this contributor, the General Editor has remarked: "Joe Snider's strength and stability as a gracious, godly man comes through in his writing. His perceptive and practical way of pointing the way to truth inspires students of God's Word."

THE GIFT
THAT KEEPS ON GIVING

Who doesn't like presents? Whether they come wrapped in colorful paper and beautiful bows, or brown paper bags closed and tied at the top with old shoestring. Kids and adults of all ages love getting and opening presents.

But even this moment of surprise and pleasure can be marked by dread and fear. All it takes is for these words to appear: "Assembly Required. Instructions Enclosed." How we hate these words! They taunt us, tease us, beckon us to try to challenge them, all the while knowing that they have the upper hand. If we don't understand the instructions, or if we ignore them and try to put the gift together ourselves, more than likely, we'll only assemble frustration and anger. What we felt about our great gift—all the joy, anticipation, and wonder—will vanish. And they will never return, at least not to that pristine state they had before we realized that *we* had to assemble our present with instructions *no consumer* will ever understand.

One of the most precious gifts God has given us is His Word, the Bible. Wrapped in the glory and sacrifice of His Son and delivered by the power and ministry of His Spirit, it is a treasured gift—one the family of God has preserved and protected for centuries as a family heirloom. It promises that it is the gift that keeps on giving, because the Giver it reveals is inexhaustible in His love and grace.

Tragically, though, fewer and fewer people, even those who number themselves among God's everlasting family, are opening this gift and seeking to understand what it's all about and how to use it. They often feel intimidated by it. It requires some assembly, and its instructions are hard to comprehend sometimes. How does the Bible fit together anyway?

What does Genesis have to do with Revelation? Who are Abraham and Moses, and what is their relationship to Jesus and Paul? And what about the works of the Law and the works of faith? What are they all about, and how do they fit together, if at all?

And what does this ancient Book have to say to us who are looking toward the twenty-first century? Will taking the time and energy to understand its instructions and to fit it all together really help you and me? Will it help us better understand who we are, what the future holds, how we can better live here and now? Will it really help us in our personal relationships, in our marriages and families, in our jobs? Can it give us more than just advice on how to handle crises? the death of a loved one? the financial fallout of losing a job? catastrophic illness? betrayal by a friend? the seduction of our values? the abuses of the heart and soul? Will it allay our fears and calm our restlessness and heal our wounds? Can it really get us in touch with the same power that gave birth to the universe? that parted the Red Sea? that raised Jesus from the stranglehold of the grave? Can we really find unconditional love, total forgiveness, and genuine healing in its pages?

Yes. Yes. Without a shred of doubt.

The *Spirit-Filled Life Bible Discovery Guide* series is designed to help you unwrap, assemble, and enjoy all God has for you in the pages of Scripture. It will focus your time and energy on the books of the Bible, the people and places they describe, and the themes and life applications that flow thick from its pages like honey oozing from a beehive.

So you can get the most out of God's Word, this series has a number of helpful features. Each study guide has no more than fourteen lessons, each arranged so you can plumb the depths or skim the surface, depending on your needs and interests.

The study guides also contain six major sections, each marked by a symbol and heading for easy identification.

WORD WEALTH

The WORD WEALTH feature provides important definitions of key terms.

BEHIND THE SCENES

BEHIND THE SCENES supplies information about cultural beliefs and practices, doctrinal disputes, business trades, and the like that illuminate Bible passages and teachings.

 AT A GLANCE

The AT A GLANCE feature uses maps and charts to identify places and simplify themes or positions.

 BIBLE EXTRA

Because this study guide focuses on a book of the Bible, you will find a BIBLE EXTRA feature that guides you into Bible dictionaries, Bible encyclopedias, and other resources that will enable you to glean more from the Bible's wealth if you want something extra.

 PROBING THE DEPTHS

Another feature, PROBING THE DEPTHS, will explain controversial issues raised by particular lessons and cite Bible passages and other sources to which you can turn to help you come to your own conclusions.

 FAITH ALIVE

Finally, each lesson contains a FAITH ALIVE feature. Here the focus is, So what? Given what the Bible says, what does it mean for my life? How can it impact my day-to-day needs, hurts, relationships, concerns, and whatever else is important to me? FAITH ALIVE will help you see and apply the practical relevance of God's literary gift.

As you'll see, these guides supply space for you to answer the study and life-application questions and exercises. You may, however, want to record all your answers, or just the overflow from your study or application, in a separate notebook or journal. This would be especially helpful if you think you'll dig into the BIBLE EXTRA features. Because the exercises in this feature are optional and can be expanded as far as you want to take them, we have not allowed writing space for them in this study guide. So you may want to have a notebook or journal handy for recording your discoveries while working through to this feature's riches.

The Bible study method used in this series revolves around four basic steps: observation, interpretation, correlation, and application. Observation answers the question, What does the text say? Interpretation deals with, What does the text mean?—not with what it means to you or me, but what it meant to its original readers. Correlation asks, What light do other Scripture passages shed on this text? And application, the goal of Bible study, poses the question, How should my life change in response to the Holy Spirit's teaching of this text?

If you have used a Bible much before, you know that it comes in a variety of translations and paraphrases. Although you can use any of them with profit as you work through the *Spirit-Filled Life Bible Discovery Guide* series, when Bible passages or words are cited, you will find they are from the New King James Version of the Bible. Using this translation with this series will make your study easier, but it's certainly not necessary.

The only resources you need to complete and apply these study guides are a heart and mind open to the Holy Spirit, a prayerful attitude, and a pencil and a Bible. Of course, you may draw upon other sources, such as commentaries, dictionaries, encyclopedias, atlases, and concordances, and you'll even find some optional exercises that will guide you into these sources. But these are extras, not necessities. These study guides are comprehensive enough to give you all you need to gain a good, basic understanding of the Bible book being covered and how you can apply its themes and counsel to your life.

A word of warning, though. By itself, Bible study will not transform your life. It will not give you power, peace, joy, comfort, hope, and a number of other gifts God longs for you to unwrap and enjoy. Through Bible study, you will grow in your understanding of the Lord, His kingdom and your place in it, and those things are essential. But you need more. You need to rely on the Holy Spirit to guide your study and your application of the Bible's truths. He, Jesus promised, was sent to teach us "all things" (John 14:26; cf. 1 Cor. 2:13). So as you use this series to guide you through Scripture, bathe your study time in prayer, asking the Spirit of God to illuminate the text, enlighten your mind, humble your will, and comfort your heart. He will never let you down.

My prayer and goal for you is that as you unwrap and begin to explore God's Book for living His way, the Holy Spirit will fill every fiber of your being with the joy and power God longs to give all His children. So read on. Be diligent. Stay open and submissive to Him. You will not be disappointed. He promises you!

Lesson 1/A Song of Wisdom

Songs!

Songs do so many things in life. They celebrate happy events like birthdays and weddings. Songs motivate athletes, soldiers, and ordinary people. Songs summarize the character and aspirations of nations. Songs tell stories that keep heroes and villains alive. Songs help people mourn; songs help them dance. Songs help us worship.

Songs touch our emotions before they touch our thoughts. Perhaps that's why so many songs sing of romance. The music of youth is obsessed with finding, keeping, and losing love. Country music resonates with love gone bad. "Oldies but goodies" remind the middle-aged of the wonders of young love. Songs spring from the heart and touch the heart.

This doesn't mean that songs are necessarily nonrational. There are many songs that sing about life in a way that opens the eyes of the heart and mind and challenge the singer. For example, the lyrics of Peggy Lee's haunting ballad "Is That All There Is?" tell of a life dedicated to the pursuit and experience of pleasure. The repeated question of the chorus exposes the awful hollowness of this "success."

Such songs contain folk-wisdom. They picture life in emotionally powerful phrases and stories. The Israelites of the Old Testament sang songs of wisdom, too, but being inspired by God Himself they are songs of *divine* wisdom.

We're going to begin our study of the Psalms with some songs of wisdom, seeing how wisdom songs bring spiritual wisdom that leads to God. It was David who observed, "The fool has said in his heart, 'There is no God' " (Ps. 14:1). The wisdom psalms fairly shout, "There is no life and no effective living without God." Let's take a look.

WORD WEALTH

Wisdom: In Old Testament times there was a category of literature known as Wisdom. The wisdom literature of Israel was concerned with the skillful conduct of personal, familial, social, business, and political affairs.

Israel's neighbor-nations also had their wisdom literature, but it was concerned with being clever and successful. Israel's wisdom was God-centered.

Wisdom literature in the Old Testament includes Job, Proverbs, Ecclesiastes, and Song of Solomon. You can see that Solomon was the writer God inspired to write most about wisdom, but he was not the only one. His father David wrote wisdom in the Psalms. One of the wisdom psalms, Psalm 90, was written by Moses several centuries before David and Solomon. This is just one example of the fact that this collection drew from many inspired writers over many years of time.

The wisdom psalms are intended to give you insight into God and people so you will have discernment and make righteous choices. "The natural man does not receive the things of the Spirit of God, for they are foolishness to him. . . . But he who is spiritual judges all things" (1 Cor. 2:14, 15).

BEHIND THE SCENES

The Book of Psalms is a collection of five smaller groups of psalms (Psalms 1—41, 42—72, 73—89, 90—106, 107—150). The five groupings arose for usage in congregational and private worship and for preservation of the poetry of Israel's worship leaders. The earliest psalm dates to the time of Moses, and the latest ones were written after the Jews returned from the Babylonian captivity. Some time after that the Lord moved an unknown person to bring together the five subsets for the edification of His people.

Among the psalms whose authors are indicated, seventy-three belong to David. A variety of other authors wrote psalms under the Holy Spirit's inspiration. Look up one psalm from each of the following sets of psalms and record the authors' names in the blanks provided.

Psalms 42; 44—49; 84; 85; 87

Psalms 50; 73—83

Psalms 72; 127

Psalm 88

Psalm 89

Psalm 90

The psalms of wisdom you are studying were written by David, the sons of Korah, Asaph, Solomon, Moses, and unnamed authors.

WISDOM ABOUT GOD

It's God's world we want to live in skillfully, so it is reasonable to begin by considering what the wisdom psalms say about God.

Psalm 47

List the different names applied to God in this psalm.

What things do the sons of Korah say that God does?

How should God's people respond to His actions?

Psalm 50

Asaph sets this song in a courtroom setting. What judicial activities does God perform in this psalm? (vv. 6, 7)

What does God call as the jury to hear the trial? (vv. 1, 4)

What group is on trial in verse 5?

What complaint is made against them? (vv. 5–13)

What response does God want from this group? (vv. 14, 15)

What group is on trial in verse 16?

What complaint is made about them? (vv. 16–20)

What wrong conclusion do the wicked reach about God? (v. 21)

What judgments will fall on the guilty? (vv. 2, 3, 22)

Who will be declared innocent? (vv. 14, 15, 23)

BEHIND THE SCENES

The Psalms use poetic expressions unique to them in the Bible. The usual name for Jerusalem in the Psalms is *Zion,* a name going back to the days of David's conquest of the Jebusite city on the hill named Zion (2 Sam. 5:6–9). The name *Zion* is used in the Psalms to denote Jerusalem as the city of God, and it symbolized divine activity in the world.

Psalm 90

How does God relate to the flow of time? (vv. 2, 4)

How does humankind's relationship to time compare to God's relationship to time? (vv. 1, 5, 6)

What do you think Moses meant by "numbering our days"? (v. 12)

How will numbering our days give us a heart of wisdom?

How will numbering our days affect our attitude toward sin? (vv. 7–11)

How will numbering our days lead to joy and gladness? (vv. 13–17)

What do you think Moses meant when he said, "LORD, You have been our dwelling place in all generations"? (v. 1)

 FAITH ALIVE

What is there in Psalms 47, 50, and 90 about God that makes you want to "clap your hands," "shout to God with the voice of triumph," and "praise the LORD with [your] whole heart"? (Ps. 47:1; 111:1)

If the Lord does not return soon and He grants you seventy or even eighty years of life (Ps. 90:10), what would you like to see Him do in these areas:

Your character

Your family

Your church

WISDOM ABOUT GOOD AND EVIL

Most of the wisdom psalms contrast the righteous person and the wicked person in character and in destiny in order to show the superiority of righteousness as a way of life.

Psalm 1

There is a progression of involvement with evil in the verbs "walks," "stands," "sits" in verse 1. Paraphrase each of these expressions:

"walks . . . in the counsel of the ungodly"

"stands in the path of sinners"

"sits in the seat of the scornful"

In what ways are associating with the wicked and delighting in the Word of God opposites of one another? (vv. 1, 2)

Explain the metaphor of the tree planted by the rivers of water used to describe the righteous person (v. 3).

Explain the metaphor of the chaff blown by the wind used to describe the ungodly person (v. 4).

Psalm 14

The fool who says in his heart, "*There is* no God" (v. 1), is not merely denying God's existence philosophically. He may be denying God's existence by the way he lives. What behaviors noted in Psalm 14 are foolish ways of acting like God doesn't exist?

How does David say that the righteous person benefits from his confidence in God's existence? (vv. 5–7)

Psalm 15

Psalm 15 is not about what God expects people to do to be saved from their sins. The psalm is about enjoying close fellowship with God.

In Old Testament times high standards of personal holiness were required of someone who wanted to remain in the presence of the Lord, which was represented by the ark of God in its tabernacle (1 Chr. 15:1). In the church only people with high standards of personal holiness enjoy intimacy with God. Psalm 15 is a signpost on the road along which the Holy Spirit yearns to lead each believer in Jesus.

Separate the righteous behaviors of Psalm 15 into those stated as things to do and those stated as things not to do.

Positive   Negative

WORD WEALTH

The fear of the Lord (Ps. 15:4) is not dread of God that causes a person to avoid Him in expectation of a lightning bolt from the blue. At the same time, the fear of the Lord is more than respect or reverence of Him. God is all-powerful. His might could squash a human like a bug. He is perfectly righteous and holy. He is capable of both an anger toward and a mighty wrath for sin.

People in the Bible who saw a manifestation of God uniformly fell down before Him until He said, "Fear not" (Ex. 3:3–6; Luke 5:8–10; Rev. 1:17). Recognize the awesome power and holiness of your compassionate heavenly Father. Realize that our very existence depends on His mercy and love. Rejoice that He still says, "Fear not," and invites us to come before Him with boldness.

Try categorizing these righteous behaviors another way. Give a label to the contents of each verse. Verse 3 is done for you as an example.

v. 2

v. 3   Righteous speech

v. 4

v. 5

Psalm 37

BEHIND THE SCENES

Psalm 37 is one of several alphabetical psalms (Ps. 9 and 10 together; 25; 34; 37; 111; 112; 119; 145). In Hebrew each succeeding verse begins with the next letter of the alphabet. The Hebrew alphabet has 22 letters, so these psalms should have 22 verses. In Psalm 37 every other Hebrew line begins alphabetically, but there aren't 44 verses because some of the English verses are so long they break the pattern.

Psalm 119 is the most remarkable alphabetical psalm. Every one of the first eight verses begins with the first letter of the Hebrew alphabet. Every one of the second eight verses begins with the second letter of the Hebrew alphabet, and so on through the twenty-second letter and the one hundred seventy-sixth verse. (This approach was a neat aid to memorizing these songs.)

The alphabetical psalms tend to be wisdom psalms. Even their structure teaches the orderliness of life lived in God's world according to God's ways.

Read through Psalm 37 and collect reasons not to be envious of the prosperity of the wicked.

Read through the psalm and jot down benefits from trusting and delighting in the Lord.

Read through the psalm again and describe the righteous person.

Psalm 94

The psalmist wanted the Lord to punish the proud and wicked (vv. 1, 2).

Summarize the psalmist's lament in verses 3–7.

Why was the psalmist sure the Lord is fully aware of the deeds of the wicked? (vv. 8–11)

How does the Lord preserve the righteous and punish the evildoer? (vv. 12–23)

Psalm 112

In this psalm the Holy Spirit calls God's children to praise the Lord for His marvelous blessings on them.

Whom does God bless? (v. 1)

What blessings does the psalmist say come from God? (vv. 2–4)

Describe the blessed man (vv. 5–9).

How do the wicked feel about the prosperity of the righteous? (v. 10)

FAITH ALIVE

How can you improve your meditation on and delight in the Word of God? (Ps. 1:2)

How can you improve your trust and rest in the Lord? (Ps. 37:3, 5, 7)

What aspects of modern life and society sometimes make you feel like the wicked are taking over without opposition from God? (Ps. 94:3–7)

Write a prayer of confidence in the Lord based on Psalms 94 and 112 about the issues you raised in the preceding question. Take some time and ask the Holy Spirit to give you real discernment and insight into how our righteous heavenly Father looks at wickedness in our world.

WISDOM ABOUT THE FAMILY

Two of the wisdom psalms speak about the family. They are among the songs of ascent that pilgrims bound for Jerusalem sang as they climbed the hills to the city. It's interesting that the Lord wanted His people reflecting on their own families as they approached His house.

Psalm 127

What are some vain ways people try to build families and

communities while ignoring the Lord? How do they end up exhausted and frustrated? (vv. 1, 2)

How did Solomon describe children in a family? (vv. 3–5)

How do godly children vindicate their parents in the presence of the parents' enemies? (v. 5)

Psalm 128

The blessing of God extends to the family of the parent who fears the Lord and walks in His ways (vv. 1–6).

When you are living in harmony with God's Spirit and His ways, how will this affect your relationship to your job? (v. 2)

When you live in harmony with God's Spirit and His ways, how will this affect your family? (vv. 3, 4)

When you live in harmony with God's Spirit and His ways, how will this affect the quality of your advanced years? (vv. 5, 6)

Lesson 2/A Song of Creation

In Genesis God spoke the world and its universe into existence, but the poets of the Bible loved to sing about the Lord's creative acts and about His handiwork. Reflection on God as Creator helps us as worshipers to reverence His great power and to marvel in gratitude that He turns from the immensity of the cosmos to care about what happens to us as individuals today in the relatively small details of our personal lives.

REJOICE IN GOD'S WORLD

Psalm 104

 ## AT A GLANCE

God engaged in His creative acts because the earth was "without form, and void" (Gen. 1:2). The first three days of creation addressed the formlessness of the world, and the second three days addressed its emptiness. God's work on days one, two, and three created three "forms," while His work on days four, five, and six filled the forms with meaning.

FORM	FILLING
Day One — Light	Day Four—Sun, Moon, and Stars
Day Two — Sea and Sky	Day Five — Fish and Birds
Day Three — Land and Sky	Day Six — Animals and People .

God's creation is artistically balanced. It is no wonder that the poets of the Bible wanted to sing about it. Psalm 104 focuses on the first three days, the creation of the three forms, and weaves the details of the populating of the forms in here and there.

DAY	GENESIS 1	PSALM 104
1	vv. 2–5	v. 2
2	vv. 6–8	vv. 3–6
3	vv. 9–13	vv. 7–18
4	vv. 14–19	vv. 19–23
5	vv. 20–23	vv. 12, 17, 25, 26
6	vv. 24–31	vv. 11, 14, 15, 18, 20–23

In verses 1–4, the psalmist described the heavens as the clothing and dwelling of God. In your own words, state the poet's imagery.

In verse 6, the psalmist says that the early earth was clothed. How was it clothed?

How does the Lord control the waters? What does He command water to do? (vv. 5–13)

For what purposes did the Lord create plants and trees? (vv. 14–18)

What functions do the moon and sun serve in God's creation? (vv. 19–23)

What things do verses 24–30 teach about God's sustaining His creation?

What responses should the glory of God shown by creation produce in His children? (vv. 31–35)

Psalm 33:1–9

What characteristics of the giver make praise beautiful and pleasing to the Lord? (vv. 1–5)

In what ways is praise of God to be as carefully crafted as God's creation of the world? (vv. 2–4, 6, 7)

By what means did God create the world? (v. 6) Keep in mind that Hebrew, like many other languages, uses the same word for "breath" and "spirit."

BEHIND THE SCENES

Notice the reference to the sea in verse 7. The Hebrew people, who lived in the hills, were fascinated by the ocean. Watch for emphasis on the seas as a symbol for God's control over the wildest part of His creation in the rest of the psalms in this lesson.

What is the basis for the fear and awe referred to in verse 8?

FAITH ALIVE

Psalm 104:34 invites meditation on God's creative activity. Read Genesis 1 and Psalms 33 and 104. Spend time alone with God rehearsing His wondrous deeds back to Him in praise. Listen to what He says to you as your Creator. Write out your final thoughts after meditating about the creation.

GOD'S WORLD REJOICES IN HIM

The Hebrew poets recognized that the heavens and earth obey the Lord without question. Of God's creatures only man rebels against his Maker. We can learn obedience by observing the workings of nature.

Psalm 29

What are "the mighty ones" (v. 1) to credit to the Lord? (vv. 1, 2) (The "mighty ones" are either powerful men or the angels of heaven—perhaps both.)

In your Bible underline all of this psalm's uses of the phrase "the voice of the LORD." List the verses in which you found these words.

What natural phenomenon does David call "the voice of the LORD" in verses 3 and 4? Where does it occur, and how does this setting enhance the majesty of God?

What disasters of nature might be described in verses 5–7? Lebanon and Sirion (usually called Hermon) are 10,000-foot mountain ranges to the north of Israel.

What does God's control of these displays of nature reveal about Him?

The events alluded to in verses 5–7 also affect the wilderness (vv. 8, 9). What do they cause?

What glory of the Lord (v. 9) is shown by the Lord's voice at work at sea, in the mountains, and in the wilderness?

How can knowledge that the Lord reigns forever as He ruled over the great flood of Noah's day give you a sense of strength and peace? (vv. 10, 11)

Psalm 65

This is a thanksgiving psalm composed by David for worshipers gathered at Jerusalem (Zion) to fulfill their vows (v. 1). In it David supported his assertions about the praise due God (vv. 1–3) by describing His mighty control of all creation (vv. 5–8). Then David's assertion about the blessedness of the saved (v. 4) is illustrated by God's bountiful control of the rains and the harvest (vv. 9–13).

In verses 1–3 what actions of God demonstrate that He is owed praise by His people?

While verses 1–3 provide intimate reasons for loving God, verses 5–7 give global reasons for being in awe of Him. Praise is inspired by love and awe. What are the bases of awe in verses 5–7?

In verse 7, David used the restless seas as a metaphor for the turmoil of the masses of people who don't know God. Go back to Psalm 93:3, 4. What would these verses be saying about God if the sea represents rebellious people?

What are the blessings of being in the presence of the Lord? (v. 4)

What are the blessings of living obediently in the creation of the Lord? (vv. 9–13)

What expressions in verses 9–13 suggest the gentleness of God in His blessing in contrast to His brute strength in controlling the seas?

What expressions in verses 9–13 suggest the joy of the cultivated ground in contrast to the rage of the sea?

PEOPLE AS GOD'S CREATION

The psalmists were certain of the Lord's absolute control of His creation when they sang of the heavens, the earth, the sea, and the birds, fish, and animals. When the poets sang about people, the apex of God's creative work, a note of discord sounded. Sin has marred the beauty of God's perfect universe. Man the rebel, designed to be king of all else God made, is an enigma. Depending on how humans relate to God, they are the glory or the shame of all He made.

Psalm 24

There are three parts to this psalm. In verses 1 and 2 David briefly describes the Lord's authority over His creation in much the same language used in the psalms in the previous section of this study. In verses 3–6 David describes in detail reminiscent of Psalm 15 the character of people who have prepared themselves for the presence of God. Finally, in verses 7–10 David describes the triumphant entry of the Lord into the midst of His prepared people.

Summarize verse 1 into one nonpoetic sentence.

Why do the seas figure so prominently in this statement about God's creation? Look at Genesis 1:2, 6–10 and Psalm 104:5–9 in forming your answer.

BEHIND THE SCENES

In verse 3 "the hill of the LORD" was Zion, and "His holy place" was the tent in which David had placed the ark of the covenant (1 Chr. 15:1). The tabernacle was still at Gibeon (1 Chr. 16:39–40). There the high priest offered the sacrifices until Solomon built the temple.

To approach the Creator God requires a certain character. In Psalm 24:4 what parts of a person are stated or implied (by the verb "sworn") as needing to be holy?

What aspects of a person's character are represented by these parts?

Verse 5 makes clear that these character attainments do not earn salvation but are the achievements of one who already knows "the God of his salvation." What does the one who "may ascend into the hill of the LORD" and "may stand in His holy place" receive from the Lord? (v. 5)

David envisioned the nation of Israel prepared in character suitable to approach the Creator God. He then envisioned the Lord coming through the gates into the city of Jerusalem, made everlasting by the presence of the "King of glory" (Ps. 24:7–10). Look through the first six verses of the psalm and find at least two sources of glory for this King of glory. What are they?

What effect is created by the poetic device of repeating the herald's call to the gates to lift up their heads? What kind of voice would this call be made in?

WORD WEALTH

"The LORD of hosts" is a title given to God as the Commander of the angelic armies of heaven. He cannot be defeated in battle. When He intercedes for His children, not only is their victory certain, but their security in the course of the conflict is guaranteed. The logic of Psalm 24 is that when the Creator God who has all power comes into the midst of people yielded and consecrated to His Spirit's control, He makes a grand entrance with all His angels as Lord of all.

Psalm 8

Is humankind basically good or basically evil? That is a loaded question because of the word *basically*. Every person has inherited a sin nature and participates in the fallenness of humankind. Psalm 8 reminds us that by design humankind is very good. It's just that every production model is fatally flawed and subject to a recall by the Designer who has paid to have every individual made like new. It's a pity that most people scoff at God's "recall notices" and perish unnecessarily.

In what two areas of creation has the Lord established His excellence and glory? (v. 1)

David asserted that the Lord is so mighty that He can defeat His enemies with the babbling of babies and toddlers

(v. 2). What was Jesus implying to the chief priests and scribes when He quoted this passage to them in Matthew 21:15, 16?

When God created the heavens, what did He appoint to rule over them? (Gen. 1:16–18)

When God completed the creation of the earth, whom did He appoint to rule over it? (Gen. 1:27–30)

When David compared the rulers of the heavens with the rulers of the earth, how did humans measure up? (vv. 3, 4) (The word translated "man" at the beginning of verse 4 is a poetic word that means "man in his frail human existence.")[1]

By creation, what is humankind's rank and status? (v. 5; cf. Gen. 1:26, 27)

By creation, what are humankind's God-given responsibilities? (vv. 6–8; cf. Gen. 1:28, 29)

BEHIND THE SCENES

The Hebrew poets who wrote the psalms did not follow the same rules of poetry that we do in English. For instance, they did not rhyme sounds, they rhymed ideas. The major poetic feature of the psalms is *parallelism*. The first line states an idea, and the second line says the same thing in a different way, or it states an opposing idea.

Most parallelism in the psalms is synonymous — two or more lines saying essentially the same thing. For example:

Blessed *is* the man
Who walks not in the counsel of the ungodly,
    Nor stands in the path of sinners,
    Nor sits in the seat of the scornful. (Ps. 1:1)

The last three lines say the same thing in slightly different ways.

Some parallelism is antithetical — two or more lines saying contrasting instead of comparative thoughts. For example:

For the LORD knows the way of the righteous,
But the way of the ungodly shall perish. (Ps. 1:6)

Some parallelism is synthetic — the following lines build up the first one, making it a complete thought. For example:

He shall be like a tree
    Planted by the rivers of water,
    That brings forth its fruit in its season. (Ps. 1:3)

Some verses in the psalms don't fit any of these categories, but most do. Don't get frustrated because it seems the psalms repeat themselves. That is intentional, and if you slow down and meditate on these poems, the repetition gives great emotional force to the praise and lamentation God's Spirit inspired. Remember that the Holy Spirit inspired these poetic expressions—every word! So take time to meditate on the implications of each.

---

1. Willem A. VanGemeren, "Psalms," *The Expositor's Bible Commentary,* Vol. 5 (Grand Rapids, MI: Zondervan Publishing House, 1991), 112.

Lesson 3 / A Song of Joy

We all know that happiness and joy are different, that happiness is a response to pleasant circumstances while joy in some way goes beyond our circumstances. Joy insists on remaining a bit of a mystery because joy is a response of the human spirit to the invisible world of God's Spirit. Joy is the exhilaration of your spirit produced by a glimpse of God's majesty or love.

The mountains, the ocean, or a wildflower might suddenly send a pang of joy through your heart so sweet it hurt, because, for an instant, maybe when you least expected it, your spirit sensed God's grandeur. In the midst of the endless pain of cancer, a semiconscious patient smiles because she sees through the weakening barriers of time and space to Jesus . . . and enjoys Him.

The disciplines of worship, whether in private devotions or public gatherings, should assist the spirit to rejoice in the Father, the Son, and the Holy Spirit. Scripture reading, memory and meditation, prayer and tongues, and singing and praise should become windows of the spirit through which God can show Himself and give us joy.

The psalmists were adept at moments of joy. They call us to join them. Rejoice in the Lord! Enjoy Him forever! Sing for joy!

REJOICE, GOD REIGNS

The first two psalms you will study concern the sovereign reign of God over all things. Whenever His Spirit opens the eyes of your spirit to glimpse God's total control of everything in and about your life, you will know joy.

Psalm 48

Verses 1–3 of Psalm 48 admire and praise God on the basis of the beauty and impregnable height of Zion, the city where the Lord chose to place His name. In the psalmist's mind, the city Jerusalem represented the entire covenant people of God. The writer of Hebrews extended the Zion concept to mean the glorious church of Jesus Christ (12:22–24), and the apostle John called the eternal city of God's future reign the New Jerusalem (Rev. 21).

How was God's greatness shown by the physical geography of Jerusalem? (Ps. 48:1–3)

How is God's greatness shown by the spiritual setting of the church? (Heb. 12:22–24)

Psalm 48:4–7 tells how various kings who had planned to attack Jerusalem changed their minds when they saw how inaccessible it was. The warlike spirit of the armies was shattered like wrecked ships. The enemies left in shame and fear. They could not touch the Lord's city and His people. Verse 8 is the psalmist's testimony that he had heard about armies frustrated by the Lord in the past and that he had actually seen it in his lifetime.

 FAITH ALIVE

Recall a story you have heard from the history of your church or from church history in general that testifies to how God frustrated Satan's attempts to destroy His church.

Describe an incident you have witnessed in which God frustrated an attack by evil people on His people.

In Psalm 48:9–14 the sons of Korah invite the worshipers in the temple to walk around Jerusalem and see for themselves what a strong fortress the city was. What physical defenses protected Jerusalem?

How were the residents of Jerusalem to respond to their protection by the Lord? (vv. 13, 14)

FAITH ALIVE

What spiritual fortifications protect the church of Jesus Christ?

How should we respond to the Lord's sovereign protection of us?

Psalm 135

Psalm 135 breaks into five sections. The first section (vv. 1–4) and the fifth section (vv. 19–21) begin and end the psalm with praise to the Lord. The second section (vv. 5–7) and the fourth section (vv. 15–18) contrast the Lord as Creator of all with the idols as things created by people. The middle section (vv. 8–14) tells how the Lord saved and kept His people Israel.

What response to the Lord did the psalmist appeal for in verses 1–4?

How is it to be expressed?

What response did the psalmist appeal for in verses 19–21?

What do you think is the difference between praising the Lord and blessing the Lord?

Compare your thoughts with the WORD WEALTH section that follows.

 WORD WEALTH

The Hebrew verbs for "to praise" and "to bless" are usually used with about the same meaning. Both focus on bearing glad testimony to the greatness of God's character and to the faithfulness of God's involvement in the lives of His people. Both are acts of worship by those who have experienced joy because of God's character and faithfulness. Both praise and blessing also have in common the fact that their very meanings incorporate the physical expressions of extending the hand—in praiseful thanks as in confessed blessing.

When praise and blessing differ, they differ in the audience to the worship. Praise tends to be a testimony about the Lord addressed to other people. Blessing tends to be a testimony about the Lord addressed to Him. Psalm 135 calls us to praise the Lord to others and to bless Him face-to-face.

What is the Lord's status? (v. 5)

What are His accomplishments? (vv. 6, 7)

What is the status of the idols? (v. 15)

What are they unable to do? (vv. 16–18)

How did the Lord show His might in bringing Israel out of Egypt? (vv. 8, 9)

How did the Lord show His might in leading Israel into the Promised Land? (vv. 10–12)

What two functions did the Lord exercise through generation after generation to guide Israel? (v. 14)

FAITH ALIVE

How has the Lord exercised these two functions in your Christian life?

Why is it important that He does both all the time?

REJOICE! GOD SAVES US!

The God sung about in the Psalms is a Deliverer. He saves from enemies, from distresses, and from sins. The poets marveled that God Almighty who splashed the stars across the sky, the Lord of hosts who puts down and raises up nations, also is the Shepherd of unthinking, straying sheep like us.

Psalm 100

What are the ways the psalmist identified for worshiping the Lord in verses 1 and 2 and in verse 4?

Verses 1, 2   Verse 4

Draw a line from each means of worship in the first list to the one in the second list most like it. Explain why you matched the lists the way you did.

When do you have opportunities to worship God in each of these ways?

What are three things the psalmist wanted his readers to realize about the Lord in verse 3 and in verse 5?

Verse 3   Verse 5

Once again draw a line from each item in the first column to its nearest match in the second column. Explain your pairings.

 FAITH ALIVE

What significance does each of these three facts about God have for your life situation?

Psalm 122

While Psalm 100 shows us a loving Savior who shepherds His people, Psalm 122 speaks of the peace that belongs to every redeemed person. This is another psalm that rejoices in God's care for Jerusalem as the focal point of Israelite worship. Psalm 122 has prophetic significance for the future of Israel and present spiritual significance for the church of Jesus Christ as the focal point of our worship of Him.

BEHIND THE SCENES

Israelites were expected to make three annual pilgrimages to Jerusalem. The Passover was in the spring, the Feast of Firstfruits (or Pentecost) was in early summer, and the Feast of Tabernacles was in the fall. These festivals were times of sacrifice, fulfilling of vows, feasting, and worship.

The festivals were not like church services. They went on day after day, and people came and went. Worship was an individual or family activity, not a large group event. Many priests were active at once, each helping one person or family. There was no congregational leader.

Pilgrims to Jerusalem stayed in inns or private homes. In addition to worship activities they engaged in tourism. Seeing the sights of Jerusalem was important to the pilgrims, and they viewed God's blessing on Jerusalem as His blessing on all of Israel.

Psalm 122 begins from the point of view of a pilgrim newly arrived in Jerusalem. He is excited about being inside the city wall, and his excitement grows even greater when others invite him to go with them to "the house of the LORD" (v. 1).

What did the pilgrim who speaks in the psalm admire about Jerusalem in verses 3–5? ("The Testimony of Israel" is a reference to the Law of Moses, which was the basis of the government from Jerusalem.)

For what things did the pilgrim petition God in his prayer for Jerusalem? (vv. 6–9)

PROBING THE DEPTHS

Prophecy and the Future of Israel (Ps. 122:6).

There are two different positions concerning what may be expected with regard to the future of Israel. . . .

Many see a continuing and distinctive role for Israel in God's plans until the end of time. These believe that Romans 9—11 indicates that a restoration of Israel will take place ("all Israel will be saved," Rom. 11:26), and that the church needs to recognize its Jewish roots ("the root supports you," Rom. 11:18). . . .

Others, however, have seen the church replacing Israel in the plan of God because the majority of the Jewish people refused to accept Jesus as Messiah. Thus the blessings and promises addressed to Israel may now only rightly be applied to the church.[1]

Incidentally, there is a third picture; that which sees a purpose of God in both *national* Israel (today's Jews) and *spiritual* Israel (the church).

Psalm 126

Psalm 126 is one of the psalms written after the Babylonian captivity of Judah. It was written five hundred years after the time of David. There is a tone of sadness behind the joy of this song, but joy depends on God rather than on circumstances. The love for Zion shown in Psalm 126 is as great as that which David expressed in Psalm 122.

What was the initial reaction of the exiles when they returned to Jerusalem? (v. 1)

When they got over that, how did those who returned celebrate? (vv. 2, 3)

The returned exiles were in Jerusalem, but the city was in ruins and the countryside had not been cultivated for decades. Life was uncertain and dangerous. (Consult Ezra and Nehemiah.) What is the basic request in the prayer of verse 4?

How is it answered in the promises of verses 5 and 6?

 FAITH ALIVE

What spiritual principles in verses 5 and 6 apply to our service to the Lord as well as to agriculture?

Why is reaping a spiritual harvest a joy? Why do we glimpse God then?

REJOICE AND SING

The three psalms covered in this section are poems that lead us in praising the Lord. They are less concerned with telling about God than they are with exalting Him.

Psalm 95

What is the psalmist's recommended way of singing and thanksgiving in verses 1 and 2?

Why was the psalmist so exuberant about the Lord? (vv. 3–5)

What postures did the psalmist recommend to show who is God and who is human? (vv. 6, 7)

What do you think makes the difference between the exuberance of verses 1–5 and the humility of verses 6 and 7?

When might you shout before the Lord and when might you kneel?

What rebellion by the children of Israel is in mind in verses 8–11? (See Ex. 17:1–7 and Num. 20:1–13.)

How will the sorts of praise commanded in verse 1–7 prevent the kind of spiritual rebellion talked of in verses 8–11?

You may want to see how the writer to the Hebrews quoted Psalm 95:8–11 to warn his readers in Hebrews 3:3—4:10. That author pointed to the Holy Spirit as the source of this psalm (Heb. 3:7).

Psalm 96

From verses 1–3 and 7–9, make a list of ways of worshiping the Lord.

Which ones of these do you need to make "a new song" in your worship of the Lord?

From verses 4–6 and 10, make a list of reasons for praising the Lord.

Notice how the same worship themes repeat through the psalms.

What parts of nature praise the Lord? (vv. 11, 12)

Why does nature praise the Lord? (v. 13)

Psalm 150

The psalmist calls on two groups to praise the Lord. From what you have read in other psalms, who should "praise God in His sanctuary"? (v. 1)

From what you have read in other psalms, who might be the ones who should praise God "in His mighty firmament"? (v. 1)

From what you have read in other psalms, what are some of God's "mighty acts" for which He should be praised? (v. 2)

From what you have read in other psalms, what are some things that make up God's "excellent greatness"? (v. 2)

What do all of the instruments and dance add to worship that makes it powerful in telling God how grand He is and how much we love Him?

1. *Spirit-Filled Life Bible* (Nashville, TN: Thomas Nelson Publishers, 1991), 864, "Kingdom Dynamics: Prophecy and the Future of Israel."

Lesson 4 / A Song of Sorrow

Because we live in a sinful world, we experience a great deal of pain in the course of daily life. It's easy most of the time to shrug off the little hurts that annoy us, but sometimes a pain is too big to ignore, or the little pains come in such a flood that they overwhelm our defenses. Then we need to be honest with God, ourselves, and others and sing a song of sorrow.

Cancer, a runaway teenager, being fired from a job, divorce, the death of a parent, or a housefire are all examples of personal calamities that will sweep some of us off our emotional feet in the near future. Hurricanes, earthquakes, floods, AIDS, war, and famine are examples of national calamities that are sweeping nations and communities off their feet right now.

Guilt because of sin is another source of sorrow for individuals and groups. Some of the songs of sorrow concern coping with God's discipline for sin. It's not easy to accept discipline, even when we know it will ultimately help us.

Only people who don't believe in God don't wonder at those times why He didn't keep them from calamity. Only people who believe in an impersonal or disinterested God don't wonder how God can love them and not make the pain stop. Only people who believe in a powerful, active, merciful God who listens to their every concern will bother to cry out to Him in pain and expect it to make a difference.

The psalmists didn't hesitate for one minute to empty their hearts of grief and fill the ear of God with their laments. They believed in a God who wanted an honest, face-to-face and heart-to-heart relationship with His worshipers. They never saw their complaints as lack of faith or disobedience. The Holy Spirit's inspiring of these songs indicates His approval of this healthy baring of the heart before God. Contrary to some current ideas promoting fear of such forthright expression, the honesty of these worshipers, confessing their sorrows, turned complaint into songs of confidence before they were through singing. We also need to learn that sorrows thoroughly exposed to God's hearing and view lose their death grip on our hearts and souls. Let these psalms teach you how to pray, to testify, and to be still before the Lord in your sorrow.

SORROW FOR MYSELF

Many songs of sorrow concern the private woes of the psalmists. We will look at these first, because we need to know how to handle individual sadness in order to function better as a group member.

Psalm 6

David was being chastened by God for his sin. What impression about God was this chastening making on David? (v. 1)

From the petitions David addressed to God in verses 2 and 4, what else do you learn about how David felt about God's discipline?

What did David think was going to happen to him? (v. 5)

What physical symptoms was David experiencing as a result of his distress? (vv. 2, 6, 7, 8)

What do you think David meant when he said, "My soul also is greatly troubled"? (v. 3)

In verses 8 and 9, David found sudden strength and resolve. Unexpectedly God's Spirit restored his spirit and he came to three conclusions. What did David conclude about

1. sinners?

2. the Lord?

3. his enemies?

Psalm 42

This psalm consists of a lament (vv. 1–4) followed by a statement of hope (v. 5) and a second lament (vv. 6–10) followed by a second statement of hope (v. 11). The psalmist wrote from the perspective of the northern borders of Israel where streams tumbled down the sides of Mount Hermon (vv. 6, 7). He was distressed by his separation from the worship at the temple in Jerusalem (v. 4).

What symptoms of depression (a downcast soul) did this son of Korah report experiencing? (vv. 1–4, 6, 7)

Why is a panting deer a good metaphor for depression? (v. 1)

How could listening to a waterfall reinforce a depressed or melancholy state of emotions? (v. 7)

What things was the psalmist depressed about? (vv. 3, 4, 9, 10)

What was the psalmist's hope for the future? (vv. 5, 8, 11)

How did he cope in the darkness of the nighttime? (v. 8)

Psalm 77

This psalm begins with a lament (vv. 1–9), moves to a reflective section (vv. 10–15), and concludes with an affirmation of the power and guidance of God (vv. 16–20). Asaph was the writer, so we have seen songs of sorrow from all three of the major composers of the Psalms: David, the sons of Korah, and Asaph.

Describe the complaining praying of Asaph (vv. 1–3).

Did Asaph worry about being heard by God? (v. 1)

What was Asaph's predetermined response to God? (v. 2)

What were the major symptoms of Asaph's distress? (v. 4)

How did Asaph try to deal with his sorrow? (vv. 5, 6)

What were his worries? (vv. 7–9)

Even in his anguish, what truths about God began to make an impression on Asaph? (vv. 10–15)

In addition to meditation, what other remedies to distress did Asaph take? (vv. 12, 13)

In verses 16–20, Asaph recalled the miracles God performed in connection with the Exodus and wilderness wandering of Israel. What is the value of recalling God's past help during a time of distress?

SORROW FOR MY PEOPLE

The three psalms to be studied in this section are songs of sorrow written at times of national distress. They concern the destruction of Israel by Assyria in 722 B.C., the burning of the temple by the Babylonians in 586 B.C., and the deportation of Judah to Babylon after the temple was destroyed.

Psalm 80

 BEHIND THE SCENES

This psalm was written in the northern kingdom of Israel, which was dominated by the tribes of Ephraim, Benjamin, and Manasseh (v. 1) after ten of Israel's tribes had broken away from Judah and Simeon in the civil war following the death of King Solomon. In the eighth century B.C. the Assyrian army invaded Palestine, defeated and deported Israel, but was turned away by the Lord before defeating Jerusalem and Judah. Psalm 80 is a lament for Israel at the time of the invasion.

In your Bible underline all the names of God found in Psalm 80.

What is the significance of each name in its context? (See WORD WEALTH, Lesson 2, page 32 about the name "LORD of hosts.")

What was Asaph's complaint to the Lord? (vv. 4–6) Keep in mind that the cities were under siege and had no food or water.

What did Asaph desire of the Lord? (vv. 3, 7, 19)

What did the psalmist tell about Israel's history by means of the image of a transplanted vine? (vv. 8–13)

What did Asaph ask of God by a continued use of the image of the vine that He had planted? (vv. 14–16)

What promise did Asaph make for Israel if God would deliver them from Assyria? (vv. 17, 18)

Psalm 74

BEHIND THE SCENES

This psalm laments the destruction of Solomon's temple in Jerusalem when the Babylonians destroyed the city in 586 B.C. Like Psalm 80, Psalm 74 also is a song of sorrow by Asaph. Asaph was not an individual who lived hundreds of years but a family of priests who served as choirmasters in the temple. See 1 Chronicles 15:19 for reference to the original Asaph who was a contemporary of David.

The psalm contains two prayers to God to remember (vv. 1–3 and 18–23). What two groups of people did Asaph want God to do something about?

What did the Babylonians do while destroying the temple? (vv. 4–8)

What things made the psalmist feel abandoned by God? (vv. 9–11)

What things did the psalmist remember about God to give himself hope? (vv. 12–17)

Psalm 137

This psalm is set in Babylon where exiles were taken by force after Nebuchadnezzar, king of Babylon, defeated Judah and destroyed Jerusalem and the temple. Sadness and determined faith mingle in this song of sorrow.

What are the symbols for the sorrow of the exiles in verses 1, 2?

What mockery made exile extra bitter for the psalmist? (v. 3)

Why didn't the psalmist want to sing about the Lord?
(v. 4)

How do verses 5 and 6 show the psalmist's faith in God
was not destroyed with the temple?

Psalm 137 ends with a vivid prayer of vengeance against
those who destroyed or connived in the destruction of
Jerusalem. The New Testament teaches, too, that vengeance
belongs to God (Rom. 12:19), but Jesus taught that we are to
love our enemies and bless those who curse us (Matt. 5:44).
(See BEHIND THE SCENES, Lesson 12, page 140).

HOPE IN MY SORROW

While all of the songs of sorrow contain sections of hope,
some of them are predominantly hopeful. Look for clues as to
how to draw strength and confidence from God's Spirit in the
midst of troubling times.

Psalm 102

For what things does the psalmist ask in his opening
prayer? (vv. 1, 2)

Describe the psalmist's physical and emotional condition
(vv. 3–7). (The birds of verse 6 are unclean fowl that inhabit
ruins and desert places.)[1]

What is the cause of the psalmist's condition and his lament? (vv. 8–11)

What prophetic promises were the basis of the psalmist's hope? (vv. 12–18)

Whom did the psalmist hope would see the glory of Jerusalem restored as though a second Exodus had occurred? (vv. 18–22)

On what did the psalmist base his expectation that he would survive as a servant of the Lord? (vv. 23–28)

BEHIND THE SCENES

The writer to the Hebrews referred Psalm 102:25–27 to the Lord Jesus to prove His eternality (Heb. 1:10–12). This is only one of nearly 300 direct quotations of the Old Testament by writers of the New Testament. There are at least another 500 allusions to the Old Testament in the New.[2]

The Holy Spirit inspired the New Testament authors with great insight into the Old Testament. Sometimes they quoted from the Hebrew version and sometimes from the Greek version. Sometimes they depended on the literal meaning of the passage quoted, but sometimes the Spirit guided them to meanings the Old Testament authors had not foreseen.

The writer to the Hebrews referred Psalm 102:25–27 to Jesus Christ even though the psalmist wrote about God. The Spirit of God had revealed to the writer to the Hebrews that the Son had been the direct agent of God's creative work (Heb. 1:2).

Psalm 130

In what depths did the psalmist find himself? (vv. 1, 3)

How is a feeling of drowning a good metaphor for this spiritual problem?

What was the subject of the psalmist's supplication to the Lord? (vv. 2, 4)

In what ways is watching for the dawn a good analogy for waiting for deliverance from the effects of sin? (vv. 5, 6)

The psalmist addressed a message of hope to Israel. Use his for a model and write a message of hope to an unbelieving friend. Use his/her name in your message. (vv. 7, 8)

 FAITH ALIVE

About which areas of your personal and spiritual life should you be more honest with God in expressing your disappointment, frustration, and shame? You won't make much spiritual progress in these areas until you've talked them over thoroughly in a frank, child-to-Father "song of sorrow."

When you are sorrowful and want relief by meditating about God, what characteristics of His should you focus on? How has His Spirit ministered to you in the past by impressing on your heart things about God?

When you can't expect immediate relief from a situation right away, what promises for the future do you find helpful? (If this has been a problem area for you, ask your pastor or a spiritually mature brother or sister for help.)

1. Franz Delitszch, *Biblical Commentary on Psalms,* Vol. III (Grand Rapids, MI: William B. Eerdmans Publishing Company, 1968), 114.

2. Roger Nicole, "The Old Testament in the New," *The Expositor's Bible Commentary,* Vol. 1 (Grand Rapids, MI: Zondervan Publishing House, 1979), 617.

Lesson 5/A Song of Trust

Eighteen-month-old Jenny and her daddy went for a walk in the neighborhood one fine spring morning. While Daddy was looking at the buds on the trees and listening to the birds, Jenny was paying attention to more important things like the cracks in the sidewalk.

Not all the sections of concrete were on the same level, and a girl can take a nasty fall if she trips, you know. This was taking a lot of concentration, what with reaching all the way up to Daddy's hand and toddling right along to keep up with him.

Suddenly Jenny's attention was grabbed by a black, furry beast hurrying across the street right at her. It was higher than her waist, and its mouth was open. She could see its teeth.

Jenny's breath stopped with fear, and her legs quit walking and started dancing in one place. Both arms reached way up toward Daddy.

Daddy scooped Jenny up. Her arms wrapped around his neck, her shoes clamped his sides, and her face buried in his neck.

In a moment Jenny stopped quaking. In another moment she let go of Daddy, leaned way back so that she was looking upside down, hair dangling, at the object of her recent terror. "Doggie!" she squealed in delight from her perch in Daddy's arms.

THE SECURITY OF THE TRUSTING

Those who trust in the Lord enjoy security like Jenny's. It is fitting that we look at three of David's psalms, because there were so many tight places through his life in which he exercised exemplary trust in his God.

Psalm 4

There are three parts to David's opening prayer (v. 1). What was he saying to God in each part?

1.

2.

3.

What kind of people had been troubling David? (v. 2)

What warning did David give these people? (v. 3)

What spiritual advice did he give them? (vv. 4, 5)

How did David answer for himself the skeptical question at the beginning of verse 6? (vv. 6, 7)

What was the result of David's song of trust? (v. 8)

Psalm 20

This psalm was David's song of trust that the citizenry could pray for every king of Israel. The people would pray that the king would trust in the Lord as his source of strength and wisdom. However, this psalm is remarkably encouraging for all of us who aren't kings or queens.

What things were the people to pray for when the king was in trouble? (vv. 1–3)

What things did this prayer assume the king was doing? (vv. 2, 3)

What things were the people to pray for the king regularly? (vv. 4, 5)

What confidence did Israel need about the Lord's care for the king? (v. 6)

What confidence did the king need about the Lord's care for Israel? (vv. 7, 8)

Psalm 62

Whereas Psalm 20 pointed out the unreliability of technology as a source of security, Psalm 62 shows that ultimately all people will let us down, too. Only God is worthy of our complete trust and confidence.

David described his soul's trust in God (vv. 1, 2), he advised his soul to trust in God (vv. 5–7), and he urged others to trust in God (v. 8). What is the image David used three times to describe God's trustworthiness?

What meaning does this image convey to you?

What sorts of treachery will some people engage in? (vv. 3, 4)

What conclusions did David reach about putting your confidence in people and human schemes for getting ahead? (vv. 9, 10)

What things has God underlined as the reasons to trust Him? (vv. 11, 12)

This psalm does not mean that you should never depend on your family, your friends, your church, your coworkers, or others. What does it mean?

When does trusting a person become excessive and replace trusting God?

THE COMMITMENT OF THE TRUSTING

Trust in God is a choice. Too many Christians exercise weak or sporadic trust in God because they aren't committed to trusting Him. Psalms 5 and 115 are songs of trust in which the psalmists express strong commitment to God.

Psalm 5

While Psalm 4 is an evening prayer, Psalm 5 is a morning prayer. Every word is addressed to God, expressing confidence in Him.

To open Psalm 5, what did David ask of the Lord? (vv. 1, 2)

What did David promise the Lord? (vv. 2, 3)

What kinds of people displease the Lord? (vv. 4–6)

What is their fate? (vv. 4–6)

How did David avoid being one of those who displease God? (vv. 7, 8)

What were David's enemies like? (v. 9)

What did David pray for his enemies? (v. 10)

What was David's prayer for all who trust in the Lord? (v. 11)

What did David expect to happen to those who trust the Lord? (v. 12)

Psalm 115

While Psalm 5 is a song of trust by an individual, Psalm 115 is a song of trust by the nation of Israel. The opening of the psalm worships the Lord (vv. 1, 2). Most of the rest of the psalm is an affirmation by Israel of their trust in the Lord (vv. 3–8, 12, 13, 16–18b). Interspersed are three reminders to Israel to keep their trust active (vv. 8, 9, 14, 15, 18c).

How did the worshipers in Psalm 115 show their humility? (v. 1)

Why did they give glory to the Lord? (v. 1)

Notice the attributes of God in Psalm 62:11, 12. How do they compare with those in Psalm 115:1? Do you think the reasons for mentioning them are similar or different in the two psalms? Why do you think that?

Does verse 2 suggest that life was going well or badly for Israel? Explain your answer.

What was Israel's answer to the Gentiles who belittled the care given them by the Lord? (vv. 3–8)

How did the psalmist mean that idol worshipers are like their idols? (v. 8)

Give an example of a present-day false god and explain how someone devoted to it becomes like it.

Who are the three groups commanded to trust in the Lord? (vv. 9–11)

What benefits do the three groups receive from the Lord? (vv. 9–11)

What else do these three groups affirm about the Lord? (vv. 12, 13)

What is one measure of blessing by the Lord? (vv. 14, 15)

What does verse 16 have to say to the Christian who would rather go straight to heaven than struggle with trusting God in the here-and-now?

What does verse 17 say to the Christian who would rather die than trust God to take him or her through struggles?

THE REWARD OF THE TRUSTING

Those who can sing the song of trust receive a grand reward from the Lord. They receive the reward of His love and protection. They receive the satisfaction of knowing the Lord smiles on their confidence in Him.

Psalm 16

What did David desire from the Lord because of his trust in Him? (v. 1)

What was David's confident opinion about the Lord? (v. 2)

What was David's confident opinion about the Lord's saints? (v. 3)

What was David's confident opinion about idol worshipers? (v. 4)

The families of Israel found their identities in their inheritances traced back to the division of the land by lot among the twelve tribes under Joshua. What did David claim as his portion or inheritance whose boundary lines fell in pleasant places? (vv. 5, 6)

David described various features of his inheritance in the Lord in verses 7–11. What are they?

BIBLE EXTRA

Peter applied Psalm 16:8–11 in his sermon on Pentecost (Acts 2:25–31). Paul referred to verse 10 in his message at Pisidian Antioch (Acts 13:35–37). The apostles understood the last verses of Psalm 16 as messianic. Look up the two passages in Acts and explain how they reached the conclusion that David had someone more than himself in mind.

Psalm 36

WORD WEALTH

Psalm 36 begins with a section called an *oracle*. This is usually a prophetic word, and its distinctive connotation is the divine authority of the utterance. There is another Hebrew word translated "oracle" that has the notion of a burden (usually of judgment), but this is not it. David opened Psalm 36 with a divinely authoritative utterance about wicked people. His readers should pay careful attention to it.

What is wrong with the self-concept of the wicked? (v. 2)

What is wrong with the speech of the wicked? (v. 3)

What is wrong with the thinking of the wicked? (v. 4)

Psalm 36 begins like a song of wisdom, but David does not contrast the righteous with the wicked. He contrasts the Lord with the wicked as an object of trust and a source of protection.

List below from verses 5 and 6 the qualities of God and their descriptions that mark the Lord as more trustworthy than the wicked.

DIVINE QUALITY   DESCRIPTION

In verses 7 through 9, David describes the protection given by God by means of several figures of speech. What does each of these suggest about God's protection?

His wings (v. 7)

His house (v. 8)

The river of His pleasures (v. 8)

The fountain of life (v. 9)

His light (v. 9)

Contrast the reward of the trusting with the reward of the wicked (vv. 10–12).

 FAITH ALIVE

What sinful attitudes have to be relinquished so that one can trust the Lord?

Why do you think the Lord values trust so highly?

The Holy Spirit is the "down payment" (foretaste or guarantee) of the future inheritance of believers in Jesus Christ (Eph. 1:11–14). From Ephesians 3:14–21, describe the reward for trusting God that belongs to a New Testament saint.

Lesson 6/A Song of Fear

Shakespeare imagined Julius Caesar protesting with his wife Calpurnia who tried to talk him out of going to the senate on the Ides of March:

Cowards die many times before their deaths,
The valiant never taste of death but once.
Of all the wonders that I yet have heard,
It seems to me most strange that men should fear,
Seeing that death, a necessary end,
Will come when it will come.[1]

Fear does funny things to people. Fear can create a coward or a hero, because it prepares the same person to run and to fight with a single rush of adrenalin. Fear ferrets out the core of one's character and exposes it while all the normal social facades are down. See a man or woman when he or she is afraid, and you see the real person. Caesar rashly ignored reasonable cautions.

People do funny things with fear. You learn a lot about someone by noticing what he is afraid of. Some people are afraid of everything. They imagine the worst possible result from any unexpected happening and anticipate it with fear. Some people seem to fear almost nothing and enjoy physically dangerous recreation. Most people experience fear at times of physical danger for themselves or loved ones and at times of great uncertainty about the future.

The psalmists were not immune to fear, and they were not ashamed to tell God about it or to invite others to join them in appealing to God for help. We should not ignore fear as Caesar did, nor should we be afraid of fear. We should turn it over to

God. We should not live cowardly lives, hating ourselves for timidity. We should trust God enough to dare to serve Him. We should fear Almighty God alone, confident that He always tells His children, "Fear not."

A SONG OF TERROR

The two psalms you will study in this section reflect the terrors and tight places of the lives of David the king and Heman, a singer in Solomon's court. These men were not crybabies, afraid of their own shadows. They were powerful individuals facing long-standing, life-threatening situations. They were real men who acknowledged their need of the Lord to deal with fear.

Psalm 55

How did David tend to feel God was reacting to his continual praying? (v. 1)

How did David characterize his prayer campaign? (v. 2)

Verse 3 summarizes David's fear-producing problem. What is it, and how does it explain his restless praying?

What was this ongoing time of fear like for David? (vv. 4, 5)

What was his human response to this fear? (vv. 6–8)

Verses 9–11, 15, 19–21, and 23 contain David's prayers for vengeance. (See BEHIND THE SCENES, Lesson 12, page 140.) What made David's dangerous situation especially painful as well as fearful? (vv. 12–14)

What did David promise the Lord, and what was his confidence even if his prayers seemed like restless moaning? (vv. 16–18)

What is David's spiritual counsel to anyone else facing betrayal and terror? (v. 22)

What did David state he would be doing when the terror was over and his tormentors had been judged? (v. 23c)

Psalm 88

Probably the most fearful song of the heart in the Psalms is Psalm 88 by Heman the Ezrahite. Apart from one vital ray of hope, which you will discover in your study, the terror of Heman is awful.

By now you must have noticed that many psalms make their initial approach to God in the same way. What does Heman appeal for in verses 1 and 2 and 9b?

Look back through some of the psalms you have already studied in this and other lessons and list at least five that have a similar beginning.

To what did Heman compare living with his fears? (vv. 3–5)

What gave him this sensation? (vv. 4, 5, 14–18)

How long had Heman felt like this? (v. 15)

What responsibilities did Heman assign to God for his living death of terror? (vv. 6–9)

In spite of this, what was his response to God? (vv. 1, 9b)

By what name did Heman address the Lord? (v. 1) How is this name the vital ray of hope in a dark psalm?

How did Heman reason that God should deliver him from the living death of his fears? (vv. 10–12)

How could you use this approach in praying about a problem that seems to be squeezing the life out of you?

  FAITH ALIVE

Whatever the psalmists feared, they were not timid in approaching the Lord. How would your prayers change if you began them as the psalmists began their songs?

What prevents us from admitting our fears to God as the psalmists did?

What prevents us from admitting our fears to others in worship and prayer as the psalmists did?

Should our fears be a theme of public worship? Why or why not?

Can a Christian be afraid and still be filled with the Holy Spirit? Why or why not?

A SONG OF PEACE

The three psalms you will study in this section reveal the peace David experienced as the Lord relieved him of his fears. The terrors and tight places of David's life endured for long stretches of time, but the peace of God went on forever for him and can go on forever for you, too.

Psalm 27

What characteristics of the Lord offset David's fears? (v. 1)

What things had caused David's fear in the past? (vv. 2, 3)

How do David's sources of fear compare with yours?

What had happened to the sources of David's fears? (v. 2)

During the years in which the young David was pursued by King Saul and during the time of Absalom's rebellion, David was separated from the tabernacle, the sacrifices, and the annual festivals. How did David find deliverance from his fears through worship at the tabernacle? (vv. 4–6)

How had the sense of the Lord's presence helped him find peace in times of fear? (vv. 7–10)

What role did God's Word play in preparing him for God's peace in fearful times? (vv. 11–13)

What is David's final advice to all of us? (v. 14)

In what way does the command "Wait on the LORD" summarize all that David testified in Psalm 27 had happened to him on the way from fear to peace?

Psalm 56

    BEHIND THE SCENES

The heading of Psalm 56 sets it at the beginning of David's flight from Saul "when the Philistines captured him in Gath." You can read about this incident in 1 Samuel 21:10–15. It must have been a vividly frightful time because it is also the setting for Psalm 34.

Eight psalms identify themselves as products of David's flight from Saul. They are, in the probable order of their composition, Psalms 7, 59, 56, 34, 52, 57, 142, and 54.[2] Their concentration in the first half of Psalms reflects that most, but not all, of David's psalms are in the first two sections of the book (Ps. 1—41 and 42—72).

Above all else, what did David ask God for in Psalm 56? (v. 1)

What caused David's fear? (vv. 1, 2)

How were his enemies attacking him? (vv. 5–7)

How did David find peace in the face of his fearsome enemies? (vv. 3, 4, 8–11)

What was David's chief insight about the protection of God? (vv. 4, 11)

What was David's vow to God? (v. 12)

Why did this vow seem so reasonable to David? (v. 13)

What did David mean when he said that mortal men can do nothing to those who trust in God? (vv. 4, 11) Did Saul do anything to David? Did Absalom? Would Job agree with this psalm? Do you?

Psalm 142

BEHIND THE SCENES

This song of fear was written by David "when he was in the cave," according to the superscription of the psalm. There are two caves in which David hid during his flight from Saul. Psalm 142 could refer to either one of them. One was the cave of Adullam where David went when he escaped from Gath and where he gathered his band of followers (1 Sam. 22:1–5).

The second cave incident was at En Gedi in the cliffs overlooking the Dead Sea (1 Sam. 24). Saul came into the mouth of the cave not knowing that David and his troop were in the cave's interior. David spared Saul's life, and Saul temporarily quit pursuing him.

David's song of fear was not a silent, little prayer from an easy chair in his living room. How did he describe his prayer? (vv. 1, 2) How would you imagine him acting while he prayed in this cave?

What was God's qualification to help David in his fear? (v. 3a)

What were David's fears? (vv. 3b, 4)

When in your life have you felt that no one cared for your soul? (v. 4d) (If you haven't had that experience, explain what you think David must have meant by it.)

In order to replace fear with peace, what did David affirm about God? (v. 5)

In order to replace fear with peace, what did David ask God to do? (vv. 6, 7a)

In order to replace fear with peace, what did David promise God that he would do? (v. 7)

 FAITH ALIVE

The next questions are modeled on the last three questions about Psalm 142. Answer them from your entire knowledge of the Scripture and your Christian experience.

In order for the Holy Spirit to replace fear with peace in your life, what do you need to know and declare as your testimony about God?

In order for the Holy Spirit to replace fear with peace in your life, what do you need to pray about and what should you ask Him to do for you? What promises would you make in your "confession"?

In order for the Holy Spirit to replace fear with peace in your life, how should you serve Him?

1. William Shakespeare, *Julius Caesar*, II, ii, 32–37.

2. Franz Delitszch, *Biblical Commentary on Psalms*, Vol. I (Grand Rapids, MI: William B. Eerdmans Publishing Company, 1968), 407.

Lesson 7/A Song of Protection

An episode of the old television detective program *Remington Steele* was entitled "Tempered Steele." In it, Mr. Steele was hired to provide security for the Dillon Electronics Company that was losing research information through burglaries. Since he had a shady past himself, Steele decided to enlist the aid of the greatest burglar he knew—a man named Wallace.

Wallace was no longer active as a burglar and did not want to get involved, even in the prevention of a burglary. He had converted to Christianity and was running a skid row mission, but Steele convinced Wallace that the sizable fee he would earn could go a long way in underwriting the operation of the mission.

The next scene showed Wallace and the crew of security "experts" he recruited from his former associates installing an elaborate electronic security system in the Dillon mansion where the research lab was located. Mr. Steele assured a doubter that the crew members had "over seventy-five years of experience" in their field.

Wallace was convincing as a protector for Dillon Electronics for two reasons. First, he was knowledgeable. He had an almost omniscient knowledge of the criminal mind that only Steele fully appreciated. He created a fortress, a sure refuge. Second, Wallace was gentle. His demeanor inspired trust and calm inside a tense situation.

Everyone wants those two qualities in a protector. We want a protector who is absolutely dependable—knowing the tactics of our opponent—and we want a protector who is kind. Without (as Wallace) having gained His insight through a conspiratorial past, but rather knowing the tactics of our adversary, our God is such a Protector, and the Psalms reveal this.

A MIGHTY FORTRESS IS OUR GOD

David, the sons of Korah, and an anonymous singer provide the three psalms you will study to look at the absolute dependability of the Lord as your Protector. You will find that these psalms are not tied to their historical settings and are easily applicable to any reader.

Psalm 31

What phrase in verses 1 and 2 acknowledges that God is high above us and is graciously condescending when He listens to our prayers?

What are the two figures of speech David used to describe the Lord as his Protector, and what does each image suggest about God? (vv. 2, 3)

FIGURE OF SPEECH   MEANING

What was David's summary request for himself (v. 2), and what details did he add in verses 3–5?

On what bases did David trust the Lord as his rock and fortress? (vv. 6–8)

In David's prayer for mercy, what physical symptoms of distress did he mention? (vv. 9–13)

What emotional symptoms of distress did David mention? (vv. 9–13)

Who was against David, and how were they pressuring him? (vv. 11–13)

In his second expression of trust in this psalm, what was David trusting God for? (vv. 14–18)

When faced with persecution, what had been David's hasty conclusion about the Lord's care? (v. 22)

What was David's mature conclusion about the Lord's care during persecution? (vv. 19–21)

What appeals did David make to all who read his song of protection? (vv. 23, 24)

In Luke 23:46 Jesus quoted the first line of Psalm 31:5 from the cross. With what thoughts from this psalm might He have comforted Himself during His suffering?

Psalm 46

In 1529 Martin Luther wrote a hymn based on Psalm 46. It remains today as a classic musical expression of the protection of God against the forces of evil. You cannot omit a verse when you sing it, because from beginning to end it builds a continuous theme: "A Mighty Fortress Is Our God." So you can see where and how many times they occur, underline in your Bible all the different names for God in Psalm 46. List them here.

✎ WORD WEALTH

The name "God" is the Hebrew word *Elohim*, which connotes the power of God as the Creator and Sustainer of all things. "The Most High" translates the Hebrew name *Elyon*, which designates God as exalted above all human and spiritual powers.

"The Lord" is the Hebrew name *Yahweh*, which is God's personal name (Ex. 3:13–16; 34:5–7). This is the name by which God entered the covenant with Israel. It connotes faithfulness and relationship. "LORD of hosts" translates the compound Hebrew name *Lord Sabaoth*, which identies God as Commander of the armies of heaven. It is His military title as defender of the covenant people.

Finally "God of Jacob" relates the Creator, *Elohim*, with the father of the tribes of Israel. God made the nation with which He entered a covenant. He sustained Jacob's descendants.

Verses 1, 7, and 11 of Psalm 46 form a triple confession of confidence in God as Protector. Summarize what these verses say about Him.

In what sorts of calamities does the psalmist confidently expect God to protect him? (vv. 2, 3)

 BIBLE EXTRA

Psalm 46:4 speaks of a river benefiting the city of Jerusalem. There are springs of water outside of Jerusalem, but there are no rivers on that hilltop. What the sons of Korah did was use a river as a symbol of the blessings of mercy and grace that flow from the presence of God to His people.

This idea of a river flowing from the presence of the Lord to the land and people all around became an important image in the thought of the Bible. Look up the following passages and summarize their messages about the river.

Psalm 36:7, 8

Ezekiel 47:1–12

Revelation 22:1, 2

How did God function as a Protector for the city of Jerusalem? (vv. 4–6)

How does God protect in time of war? (vv. 8, 9)

How does God want His people to look to Him as their Protector? (v. 10)

Psalm 91

This psalm is filled with figurative language. Let your imagination picture the images, and you will have a better chance of capturing the vivid message the Holy Spirit gave this anonymous singer of a song of protection.

The psalmist invites his readers to "the secret place of the Most High" (v. 1) for protection. Ancient fortresses sometimes had secret chambers for security from a successful invader. What inner recesses of intimacy with God might the psalmist have in mind as "the secret place"?

Using the information in WORD WEALTH about the names of God, explain why the psalmist changed from "Most High" and "Almighty" in verse 1 to "the LORD" in verse 2.

What images for God as Protector are used in verses 1–6, and what does each tell about Him?

What images for danger are used in verses 3–13, and what aspect of risk does each represent?

What role do angels play in God's protection of His people? (vv. 11, 12; see also Ps. 103:20, 21; Matt. 18:10; Heb. 1:13, 14)

To whom does God make a personal pledge of protection? (vv. 14–16)

What does God promise? (vv. 14–16)

THE LORD IS MY SHEPHERD

This section also contains a psalm by David, a psalm by the sons of Korah, and an anonymous psalm. While there are times when we want to know that the Lord our Protector is a strong fortress, there are other times when we need to know that He is a tender, compassionate Shepherd.

Psalm 23

This is the most familiar of the Psalms because it speaks of the Lord's care and comfort in images simple enough for a child to respond to and profound enough for an adult in an awful crisis. The Lord is viewed as a shepherd of His sheep (vv. 1–4) and as a host of His feast (vv. 5, 6). The shepherd image dominates our memories of the psalm.

What are the daily wants the Shepherd provides for His sheep, and what does each represent in our lives? (vv. 2, 3)

DAILY WANT   MEANING

What is the special "want" the Shepherd provides for when necessary? (v. 4) Why is it called "the valley of the <u>shadow</u> of death"?

How did a shepherd use his rod? (v. 4; see 1 Sam. 17:34, 35)

How might the Lord use His Shepherd's rod on your behalf?

How did a shepherd use his staff (shepherd's crook)? (v. 4)

How might the Lord use His Shepherd's staff on your behalf?

In the image of a great banquet what role does each of the following play? (v. 5)

PERSON   ROLE

The Lord

David (or the reader)

The enemies

How was David honored by the Lord at the banquet? (v. 5)

How does the first half of verse 6 summarize what David presented about protection by the Lord as Shepherd and Host?

In the last half of verse 6, what does David's promise mean, and why did he make it?

If the anointing oil (v. 5) represents the Holy Spirit in His fullness on the life of a Christian, how does that help you understand verse 6?

Psalm 84

The sons of Korah addressed a song of protection to the Lord of hosts (see WORD WEALTH at Psalm 46). The psalmist assigned a military name to God, which fits the idea of protection well, but then wrote about Him in terms of gentleness. The poem captures the duality of this lesson on protection. The Lord is tough but tender when He protects His own.

The psalmist was away from the temple for an extended time. What were his thoughts on the presence of God? (vv. 1, 2)

What feelings did his recollection of a bird's nest in the temple area awaken in the psalmist? (vv. 3, 4)

BEHIND THE SCENES

The identification of the Valley of Baca (v. 6) is the subject of disagreement. Ancient versions have understood it to mean the Valley of Weeping, but some understand *Baca* to mean a tree, perhaps the mulberry (2 Sam. 5:22–25). The context of the psalm seems to support the older view. As pilgrims bound for Jerusalem pass through this exhausting desert place, their tears flow like springs. God will bless their desire to worship Him.

How did the psalmist imagine the mighty Lord of hosts caring tenderly for His pilgrims wandering in a barren land? (vv. 5–7)

The psalmist imagined the praise the pilgrims would offer the Lord when they arrived at the temple in Jerusalem (vv. 8–11). They pray for the king (the Lord's anointed) in verses 8 and 9 and glory in God's protection of all His people in verses 10 and 11.

What role did the king play in protecting the people? (v. 9)

What role did the Lord play in protecting the king and the people? (v. 11)

Describe the pilgrims' joy of verses 10 and 11.

What is your attitude toward being in the presence of the Lord in private and public worship?

Summarize the blessings the psalmist has imagined for the person who trusts in the Lord (v. 12).

Psalm 121

Imagine with the psalmist that you are walking day after day toward Jerusalem on a pilgrimage. Just in front of you looms a range of hills. All sorts of thoughts might go through your mind when you "lift up [your] eyes to the hills" (v. 1). What might some of those thoughts be?

One question the hills provoked from the pilgrim was, "From whence comes my help?" (v. 1). How did the psalmist answer that question? (v. 2)

What qualified the Lord to protect the vulnerable pilgrim? (v. 2)

What sort of protection does the Lord give? (vv. 3–6)

What sort of Protector is the Lord? (vv. 3–6)

What is the repeated word of protection in verses 3–6?

The verbs of verses 7 and 8 no longer describe the present protection of the Lord. They project His protection into the future. What protection is promised?

What is the repeated word of protection in verses 7 and 8?

Lesson 8/A Song of Thanksgiving

Mrs. Pumphrey is one of the wonderful characters who inhabit the Yorkshire Dales of James Herriot's *All Creatures Great and Small*. Mrs. Pumphrey, a wealthy widow, presided over a large house and estate with a full staff of servants. She was intelligent, committed to charitable causes, amusing, and generally capable, except for one area of her life in which she behaved quite eccentrically.

Mrs. Pumphrey had a Pekingese that she called Tricki Woo because she was certain he was descended from a long line of Chinese emperors. She attributed numerous human traits to her dog and expected her servants and friends to treat Tricki as she did. Poor Tricki got little exercise and all the rich, unhealthy food his greedy canine heart desired.

As a consequence, young veterinarian James Herriot was a frequent visitor to Barlby Grange, the Pumphrey house, to try to resurrect the moribund digestion of Tricki Woo. Mrs. Pumphrey assured James that Tricki was so grateful for his ministrations that he had adopted him as his "Uncle Herriot."

Thereafter, the veterinary office was the regular destination of assorted gifts ostensibly sent by Tricki and accompanied by notes "dictated" by the dog to his owner. Tricki's most generous gifts were his Christmas hampers, vast assortments of expensive delicacies from Fortnum and Mason's, the London-based grocers to the British crown.

Tricki Woo's generosity was an eccentric facade behind which Mrs. Pumphrey concealed her gratitude. The little Pekingese was the closest companion of this elderly woman, and it meant a great deal to her every time his health was restored. The lavish gifts she sent in the dog's name bore significance.[1]

The writers of the psalms composed songs of gratitude as gifts to the Lord. The lavishness of their songs, like the lavishness of Mrs. Pumphrey's gifts, reveals the depths of their thanksgiving for everything God had done for them.

GRATITUDE FOR GOD'S GREATNESS

The thanksgiving expressed in the Psalms begins with a realization of how great God is. None of His actions for any individual can be perceived correctly outside the context of His broader work in creation and history.

Psalm 66

How should gratitude for God's awesome works be expressed? (vv. 1, 2)

Who will praise God's awesome works? (vv. 1–4)

What awesome works in the history of Israel should inspire gratitude to God? (vv. 5–7) Look at the discussion of Psalm 114 in Lesson 2.

What awesome works in our lives should inspire gratitude to God? (vv. 8–12)

BIBLE EXTRA

The psalmist wrote, "For You, O God, have tested us; You have refined us as silver is refined" (Ps. 66:10). This powerful image of purification from moral and spiritual impurities, expressed in praise to the Lord, attracted the attention of the New Testament writers.

Peter wrote, "In this you greatly rejoice. . . that the genuineness of your faith, *being* much more precious than gold that perishes, though it is tested by fire, may be found to praise, honor, and glory at the revelation of Jesus Christ" (1 Pet. 1:6, 7). James abbreviated the image in this way: "My brethren, count it all joy when you fall into various trials, knowing that the testing of your faith produces patience" (James 1:2, 3).

What did the psalmist promise God as acts of thanksgiving? (vv. 13–15)

What did the psalmist realize would frustrate his attempts to pray or to thank God for blessing him? (v. 18)

What is the difference between sinning and repenting, on the one hand, and regarding iniquity in my heart, on the other hand? (v. 18)

Psalm 106

This remarkable song of thanksgiving narrates many of the spiritual failures of Israel. The gratitude of the psalmist is for

God's loyal love that patiently chastened and restored His wayward people. Be sure that you read the entire psalm and understand the big picture before looking at pieces of it.

For what did the psalmist call on his readers to give thanks to the Lord? (vv. 1–3)

Why is the psalmist encouraged by his recitation of God's faithfulness to His covenant people? (vv. 4–5)

What amazed the psalmist so much about the Lord's redemption of Israel from slavery in Egypt? (vv. 6–12)

In what sense did God save you "for His name's sake, that He might make His mighty power known"? (v. 8)

How did Israel rebel against the Lord during the wilderness wandering, and how did the Lord discipline them? (vv. 13–33)

REBELLION	DISCIPLINE
Ps. 106:13–15; Ex. 17:1–7	
Ps. 106:16–18; Num. 16:1–35	
Ps. 106:19–23; Ex. 32:1–14	
Ps. 106:24–27; Num. 14:1–38	

Ps. 106:28–31; Num. 25:1–9

Ps. 106:32, 33; Num. 20:1–13

How did Israel rebel against the Lord after the conquest of Canaan under Joshua's leadership? (vv. 34–39)

How did the Lord discipline them? (vv. 40–42)

Why was the psalmist thankful to God for His actions through all of this sin and discipline? (vv. 43–46)

In all likelihood, Psalm 106 was written during the seventy years when the nation of Judah was deported to Babylon as discipline for their sins. From verses 6 and 47, how was the psalmist using the past to appeal to God for Judah as a scattered people?

Why didn't the psalmist wait until the Lord restored His people before praising Him? (v. 48)

Why shouldn't you wait for the next awesome work before praising Him?

GRATITUDE FOR ANSWERED PRAYER

Many of the Psalms begin with strong appeals to the Lord to pay attention to the pleas of God's people. These appeals never arose out of any doubt that the Lord was concerned about the struggles of life. These psalms are bold advances into the presence of God. The Psalms operate on the assumption that communication with the Almighty is one of the greatest privileges mankind has, and thanksgiving for answered prayer is a theme one expects to discover there.

Psalm 41

David wrote this psalm in an unusual fashion. In verses 1–3, he blessed the Lord in anticipation of wonderful things he was sure the Lord was going to do for him. Then in verses 4–12, David recorded his prayer for these things he had already blessed the Lord for.

What did David bless the Lord for doing on behalf of the poor man? (vv. 1–3)

What is the main verb of appeal in David's prayer? (v. 4)

For what areas of his life did David make this appeal? (vv. 4–9)

How were David's enemies using his illness against him? (vv. 5–8)

To David, what was the most hurtful thing about the ringleader's attack on him? (vv. 6, 9)

What did David ask of God's mercy? (vv. 10–12)

What does David's song of thanksgiving for answered prayer in Psalm 41 suggest to you about confidence in God's response to prayers for physical healing?

Psalm 138

In this psalm, David praised the Lord for answering his prayers (vv. 1–3), promised that one day the kings of the earth will lead their peoples in praising God (vv. 4–6), and finished with a statement of confidence in the Lord's continued care (vv. 7, 8).

What things did David promise to do (vv. 1, 2a) because God had answered his prayer? (vv. 2b, 3)

Why do you think David wanted the heathen gods to hear his praise of the God who answers prayer? (vv. 1, 4)

What characteristics of God did David relate to His answering of prayer? (v. 2)

What happened to David when God answered his prayer? (v. 3b)

What result did David want his testimony before the heathen gods to have in the hearts of the Gentile kings? (vv. 4–6)

Why should it matter to idol worshipers that the true God answers the prayers of the lowly? (v. 6)

What things did David know he could pray for and receive because they were the Lord's will? (vv. 7, 8)

GRATITUDE FOR SALVATION

Ultimately thanksgiving in the Psalms becomes thanksgiving for deliverance. The Lord delivers from enemies, from diseases, and from calamities. Most glorious of all is the realization that the Lord delivers from the guilt and judgment of sin.

Psalm 18

This psalm appears in its entirety in 2 Samuel 22. Samuel recorded it as David's reflection on God's protection of his public life, beginning with his conflict with King Saul. That usage fits very well the content of the superscription of the psalm.

Psalm 18, therefore, is not about salvation from sin, but about the Lord's deliverance from difficulties. As with the other long psalms, it is a good idea to read Psalm 18 in its entirety before breaking it into pieces.

What was David's emotional response to the Lord's salvation? (v. 1)

WORD WEALTH

Love (Ps. 18:1). The Hebrew *'ahab* is remarkably similar to the English verb "to love" in that its range of meanings covers the same ideas. *'Ahab* can refer to loving God, loving one's friends, romantic love, love of ideals, love of pleasures, and so on. The participial form, *'oheb,* refers to a friend or lover. The first mention of love in the Bible is in Genesis 22:2 where Abraham loved his son Isaac.[2]

The language of the first three verses of this song of thanksgiving is like that of the psalms in another lesson. Which other type of song used these terms? (vv. 1–3)

What image for the Lord from the opening of Psalm 18 did David come back to in the final verses? (vv. 46–50)

How do all of the names for God in verses 1–3 explain David's thanksgiving in verses 46–50?

Psalm 18 begins with God's strength to save and ends with David's gratitude for salvation. Right in the middle of the psalm (vv. 20–30) is a section about the one whom the Lord delights to deliver. What was David, who certainly was not sinless, saying about himself in verses 20 through 24?

Using one or more New Testament concepts, restate what David said about the Lord in verses 25 and 26.

Verses 1–3 and 46–50 make strong statements about the Lord's protection. Verses 20–27 demand righteousness of God's people. How do verses 28–30 bring these two concepts together?

Psalm 18:4–19 uses colorful language and images to describe the Lord in action as Savior. What danger was David in? (vv. 4–6)

What is the Lord like in battle? (vv. 7–15)

What was David's deliverance like? (vv. 16–19)

Psalm 18:31–45 describes David the warrior who had the Lord at his right hand. What did the God of verses 7–15 transform David into? (vv. 31–36)

While David saw the Lord with his spirit (vv. 7–15), what did David's enemies see with their eyes? (vv. 37–42)

What happened when David fought in the Lord's strength? (vv. 43–45)

Psalm 30

The superscription of Psalm 30 connects this song of thanksgiving to the construction of David's palace (2 Sam. 5:11), but the content of the psalm is focused on spiritual issues because David viewed the palace as an evidence of God's blessing on the future (2 Sam 5:12).

How was the basis for David's rejoicing in Psalm 30:1–3 like that of Psalm 41:1–12?

What had David discovered about trouble and blessing in the life of God's saints? (vv. 4–7)

What had been the turning point for David from trouble to blessing? (vv. 8–10)

How did David reason with the Lord? (v. 9)

For what was David eternally grateful? (vv. 11, 12)

 FAITH ALIVE

How has God answered your prayers and made you grateful?

For what are you thankful with regard to your salvation from sin?

For what other things that God has done for you are you thankful?

---

1. James Herriot, *All Creatures Great and Small* (New York, NY: St. Martin's Press, 1972), chap. 13.

2. *Spirit-Filled Life Bible* (Nashville, TN: Thomas Nelson Publishers, 1991), 837, "Word Wealth: 97:10 love."

Lesson 9/A Song of God's Word

When the rest of the pirates rebelled against Long John Silver in *Treasure Island,* they signaled their displeasure with a "Black Spot." The black spot was a buccaneer notice that a council had been held and a verdict had been reached against Long John. The spot identified the nature of the business, and the word *Deposed* scrawled under the spot announced the verdict.

Long John Silver's cunning saw a way to divert the attention of his comrades from their purpose of replacing him.

"Why, hillo! look here now: this ain't lucky! You've gone and cut this out of a Bible. What fool's cut a Bible?"

"Ah, there!" said Morgan—"there! Wot did I say? No good'll come o' that, I said."

"Well, you've about fixed it now, among you," continued Silver. "You'll all swing now, I reckon. What soft-headed lubber had a Bible?"

"It was Dick," said one.

"Dick, was it? Then Dick can get to prayers," said Silver. "He's seen his slice of luck, has Dick, and you may lay to that. . . . And now, shipmates, this black spot? 'Taint much good now, is it? Dick crossed his luck and spoiled his Bible and that's about all."

"It'll do to kiss the book on still, won't it?" growled Dick, who was evidently uneasy at the curse he had brought upon himself.

"A Bible with a bit cut out!" returned Silver derisively. "Not it. It don't bind no more'n a ballad book."[1]

To Long John Silver and his treacherous comrades, the Bible was an object of superstitious respect. Only a soft-headed person would have one, but if a Bible was around, it deserved special treatment to obtain good luck and avoid bad luck.

David and the other psalmists would have been bewildered if not appalled at this sort of attitude toward the Bible. To them the Scriptures were the wonderful Word of God. It is the book about life and godliness; luck does not enter the picture.

A SONG OF PERFECTION

Psalm 19

In this beautiful poem, David sang about the revelation God makes of Himself in nature and in His Word. His revelation in nature is good; His revelation in His Word is better. In fact, it is perfect.

What do the heavens reveal about God? (v. 1) Compare Romans 1:20.

When do the heavens reveal God? (v. 2)

To whom do the heavens reveal God? (v. 3)

Where do the heavens reveal God? (v. 4)

How is the sun like a bridegroom going to his wedding? (v. 5a)

How is the sun like a strong man getting ready to run a race? (v. 5b)

What makes the sun the greatest heavenly revealer of God? (vv. 4c–6)

What is the result of God's revelation of Himself in the heavens? (see Romans 1:18–21)

The divine name associated with the revelation of the heavens is *God;* the one associated with God's Word is *Lord.* Look at WORD WEALTH under Psalm 46 in Lesson 7 on page 86 and explain why David made this name change.

 WORD WEALTH

There are eight primary terms for the Word of God used in Psalm 19 and 119 . They are used as rough synonyms, but each has its own shade of meaning. The first five terms occur in Psalm 19. They all appear in Psalm 119.

Law has the basic meaning of instruction. Its biblical sense is instruction by God about how to live in order to please Him. Law is God's instruction about reality. There is nothing arbitrary or capricious about the law.

Testimony is often synonymous with covenant. The testimony of the Lord is His arrangement with His people by which they are acceptable to Him.

Precept or *statute* (same Hebrew term) refers to the revelation of the covenant. A precept is something revealed to be guarded and obeyed.

Commandment designates an order to be obeyed. It carries the authority of the one who issued it, so God's commandments are the greatest ones.

Judgment identifies a decision by God about issues of human behavior. His judgments are not made as bad behavior emerges but were made in advance.

Statute (a different Hebrew term than "statute" or "precept" above) denotes a decree issued by the sovereign Lord. They are better than the decrees of human kings.

Word is a term about speech. The word is what proceeds from the mouth of God. It is a divine utterance.

Another Hebrew term translated "word" has the sense of promise. Men's words or promises are undependable, but God's words are sure.[2]

What things can God's Word do that the revelation of nature cannot? (vv. 7, 8, 11a)

What are some characteristics of God's Word? (vv. 9, 10, 11b)

What understanding and conviction of sin can God's Word give that the revelation of nature cannot? (vv. 12, 13)

What personal transformation did David desire from God's Word? (v. 14)

A SONG OF LOVE AND OBEDIENCE

Psalm 119

This psalm is an alphabetical psalm. See BEHIND THE SCENES in Lesson 1 under Psalm 37 on page 19 for a discussion of alphabetical psalms. There are twenty-two stanzas of eight verses in Psalm 119. Every one of the 176 verses mentions the Word of God by means of the eight common terms glossaried above and a multitude of less frequently used synonyms.

The alphabetical format of this song of God's Word imposed an artificial structure that made it difficult for the psalmist to develop a flow of thought. Consequently, Psalm 119 can seem repetitious and disjointed.

In the exercise that follows, you are given a theme for each stanza of Psalm 119. In the provided spaces, record the major lessons you find in each stanza.

Psalm 119:1–8 BLESSED ARE THE OBEDIENT

Psalm 119:9–16 WRITTEN ON MY HEART

Psalm 119:17–24 AN EYE-OPENER

Psalm 119:25–32 TRUTH OR DECEIT

Psalm 119:33–40 THE LIFE PRESERVER

Psalm 119:41–48 THE LIBERATOR

Psalm 119:49–56 COMFORT TO A SUFFERER

Psalm 119:57–64 A VOW OF OBEDIENCE

Psalm 119:65–72 LORD, TEACH ME

Psalm 119:73–80 THE LIFE-GIVER

Psalm 119:81–88 PREVENTS SPIRITUAL FAINTING

Psalm 119:89–96 BOUNDLESS, TIMELESS

Psalm 119:97–104 MAKES VERY WISE

Psalm 119:105–112 LIGHT TO MY FEET

Psalm 119:113–120 THE RIGHT PATH

Psalm 119:121–128 MORE PRECIOUS THAN GOLD

Psalm 119:129–136 GIVES DIRECTION

Psalm 119:137–144 THOROUGHLY TESTED

Psalm 119:145–152 HOPE FOR SECURITY

Psalm 119:153–160 SALVATION IN PERSECUTION

Psalm 119:161–168 SOURCE OF PEACE

Psalm 119:169–176 THEME OF MY SONG

FAITH ALIVE

What do you think was the main point David wanted to make about God's Word in Psalm 19?

How would you summarize the psalmist's attitude toward God's Word in Psalm 119?

How would you complete this statement? I love the Word of God because

Record some things the Word of God has taught you that you could not have learned if it did not exist.

Compose a prayer of gratitude to God for how He has transformed your life through His Word. Be specific about changes His Word has produced.

1. From TREASURE ISLAND by Robert Louis Stevenson (Charles Scribner's Sons, an imprint of Macmillan Publishing Company, New York, 1911). Reprinted with permission of the Publisher.

2. Willem A. VanGemeren, "Psalms," *The Expositor's Bible,* Vol. 5 (Grand Rapids, MI: Zondervan Publishing House, 1991), 185, 186, 737, 738.

Lesson 10/A Song of the Messiah

In the Old Testament anointing an object or a person with oil indicated that the object or person had been set apart by God for a special purpose. The priests and some of the prophests were anointed, but the Old Testament emphasized the anointing of kings, especially as deliverers from enemies.

David held the concept of anointing in especially high esteem. Saul had been the first man anointed king of Israel (1 Sam. 10:1). In the course of time, Saul demonstrated spiritual weakness, and the Lord anointed David to succeed him (16:13). Saul became despondent about losing the kingdom for his posterity and ruthless in his attempts to kill David and frustrate the purposes of God.

On two occasions as Saul pursued David and his band of men, David had opportunity to kill Saul. If David had listened to his advisers and killed him, David would have been spared years of exile, he would have come to the throne that much quicker, and he would have dramatically demonstrated his superiority over Saul. David could have written psalms about how the Lord had delivered his enemy into his hand and rallied the nation of Israel around himself and the Lord.

But David refused to harm Saul. Even though Saul was a moral and spiritual failure who was destined to lose the throne, David's stance was "I will not stretch out my hand against my lord, for he *is* the LORD's anointed" (1 Sam 24:10; see also 24:6; 26:9, 11, 16, 23). Only the Lord could terminate His special ordination.

It isn't surprising that David and the prophets applied the concept of anointing to the future Ruler of God's people, the Ruler who would reign forever over all the earth with justice and righteousness for all, the Ruler who was somehow Son of

David and Son of God. The Hebrew verb "to anoint" is *mashach*; the noun for "anointed one" is *mashiach*, which comes into English as *Messiah*. In Greek it is *christos* from which the title-name *Christ* comes.

Sing with the psalmists a song of the Messiah.

 AT A GLANCE

THE CHRIST OF THE PSALMS		
Psalm	**Portrayal**	**Fulfilled**
2:7	The Son of God	Matthew 3:17
8:2	Praised by children	Matthew 21:15,16
8:6	Ruler of all	Hebrews 2:8
16:10	Rises from death	Matthew 28:7
22:1	Forsaken by God	Matthew 27:46
22:7, 8	Derided by enemies	Luke 23:35
22:16	Hands and feet pierced	John 20:27
22:18	Lots cast for clothes	Matthew 27:35,36
34:20	Bones unbroken	John 19:32, 33,36
35:11	Accused by false witnesses	Mark 14:57
35:19	Hated without cause	John 15:25
40:7, 8	Delights in God's will	Hebrews 10:7
41:9	Betrayed by a friend	Luke 22:47
45:6	The eternal King	Hebrews 1:8
68:18	Ascends to heaven	Acts 1:9–11
69:9	Zealous for God's house	John 2:17
69:21	Given vinegar and gall	Matthew 27:34
109:4	Prays for enemies	Luke 23:34
109:8	His betrayer replaced	Acts 1:20
110:1	Rules over His enemies	Matthew 22:44
110:4	A priest forever	Hebrews 5:6
118:22	The chief stone of God's building	Matthew 21:42
118:26	Comes in the name of the Lord	Matthew 21:9

This chart compiles many of the messianic passages of the Psalms. You will study most of them in this lesson, but there are others you may want to look up on your own.[1]

A SONG OF MESSIANIC POWER

The psalmists and the prophets did not foresee primarily a suffering Messiah. They saw the King of kings and Lord of lords, Ruler of all the earth, and they were right. The Christ of Revelation and the Messiah of Psalms 2 and 110 are identical.

Psalm 110

This is the most quoted psalm in the New Testament. Jesus used it (Luke 20:42), the apostles referred to it (Acts 2:34, 35), and the writer to the Hebrews was especially fond of it (Heb. 1:13; 5:6).

What do verses 1 and 2 say about the Messiah as God's appointed King?

What do verses 3 and 4 say about the Messiah as God's appointed Priest and about those who will serve Him?

What do verses 5–7 say about the Messiah as God's appointed Judge?

What point did Jesus make about the Messiah from Psalm 110:1? (Matt. 22:41–46; Mark 12:35–37; Luke 20:41–44)

What point did Peter make about Jesus from Psalm 110:1? (Acts 2:33–36)

What point did the writer to the Hebrews make about Jesus from Psalm 110:4? (Heb. 5:5–11; 6:19—7:28)

Psalm 2

This Psalm captures the militant tone of the time when the Messiah will set up His kingdom and crush those who oppose Him. Verse 7 is quoted extensively in the New Testament. Verses 1–3 are not set in the future like verses 4–9. What tends to be the attitude of nations and rulers toward the Lord and His Messiah at all times and all places? (vv. 1–3)

In the Lord's time what will be His response to the rebellious nations and rulers? (vv. 4–6)

What is contained in the Lord's decree concerning the Messiah? (vv. 7–9)

What is the advice of this anonymous psalmist to the kings and nations of all times and places? (vv. 10–12)

What point did Paul make about Jesus from Psalm 2:7? (Acts 13:33, 34)

What two conclusions about the Messiah did the writer to the Hebrews draw from Psalm 2:7? (Heb. 1:5; 5:5)

 FAITH ALIVE

What is David's mood of worship in Psalm 110?

What is the mood of worship expressed in Psalm 2?

How can you express these attitudes of worship in your adoration of Jesus as the Messiah, mighty King of all the earth?

What implications does Psalm 2:10–12 have for the leaders of your country in the moral and spiritual issues facing them today?

A SONG OF MESSIANIC GLORY

Psalms 45 and 72 are royal psalms that express God's ideal for the Davidic dynasty. The ideas of both psalms eventually extend beyond the human realm into dimensions of the messianic kingdom. The sons of David give way to the Son of David.

Psalm 72

The nation of Israel expected great things of Solomon. He was the son of David, and his reign was the golden age of Israel. The kingdom reached its greatest size, experienced peace and prosperity, and was a power looked to by the nations all around. It was natural to wonder if the eternal promises made by the Lord to David (2 Sam. 7:12–16) would be fulfilled by Solomon. The Lord inspired Solomon to write Psalm 72 to show that the Messiah's kingdom was still future.

What will be the major characteristics of the messianic kingdom? (vv. 1–4, 12–14)

What will be the extent of the messianic kingdom? (vv. 5–11)

What will be the results of the messianic kingdom? (vv. 15–17)

How does the praise of verses 18 and 19 summarize the mood of Psalm 72 (and the second grouping of psalms, Psalms 42—72)?

What characteristics of the king described in Psalm 72 could be fulfilled only by the Messiah?

Psalm 45

The sons of Korah wrote this psalm as a wedding song at the marriage of one of the kings of Judah. The thoughts of the song quickly soar into the eternal and it becomes a poem of the Messiah and His bride, the church.

What qualities make the Messiah excellent? (vv. 2–5)

Why has God chosen to anoint the Messiah? (vv. 6, 7)

What point did the writer to the Hebrews make from Psalm 45:6, 7? (Heb. 1:8, 9) You may want to read the whole first chapter of Hebrews to catch the flow of thought.

What was the royal bride like? (vv. 9, 13–15)

What advice did the psalmist give the royal bride? (vv. 10–12)

What parallels can you draw between the royal bride and the church of Jesus Christ?

What will be the result of the Messiah's marriage? (v. 17)

FAITH ALIVE

What was Solomon's mood of worship in Psalm 72?

What was the sons of Korah's mood of worship in Psalm 45?

How can you express these attitudes of worship in your adoration of Jesus, the Messiah, glorious in His character?

A SONG OF MESSIANIC SUFFERING

The messianic psalm that startles those who read it for the first time is Psalm 22. David began to describe his own torments at a time of abandonment, but he went far beyond his experience under the inspiration of the Holy Spirit to describe the anguish of One who would live a millennium later.

Psalm 22

What was the Messiah's complaint? (vv. 1, 2)

Why do you think Jesus quoted Psalm 22:1 from the cross? (Matt. 27:45, 46; Mark 15:33, 34)

What was the Messiah's hope? (vv. 3–5)

  BEHIND THE SCENES

"Establishing" God's Throne (Ps. 22:3). The Psalms were the praise hymnal of the early church, and as such are laden with principles fully applicable for New Testament living today. Few principles are more essential to our understanding than this one: the <u>presence</u> of God's kingdom power is directly related to the practice of God's <u>praise.</u> The verb "enthroned" indicates that wherever God's people exalt His name, He is ready to manifest His kingdom's power in the way most appropriate to the situation, as His rule is invited to invade our setting.

It is this fact that properly leads many to conclude that in a very real way, praise prepares a <u>specific</u> and <u>present</u> place for God among His people. Some have chosen the term "establish His throne" to describe this "enthroning" of God in our midst by our worshiping and praising welcome. God awaits the prayerful and praise-filled worship of His people as an entry point for His kingdom to "come"—to enter, that <u>His</u> "will be done" in human circumstances.[2]

What public humiliation did the Messiah endure? (vv. 6–8)

What was the Messiah's personal relationship with God? (vv. 9–11)

What were the Messiah's enemies like? (vv. 12, 13, 16, 20, 21)

What were the Messiah's personal sufferings? (vv. 14–20)

Read Matthew 27:32–56 and John 19:17–37. Point out the fulfillments of Psalm 22 in the crucifixion narratives.

What is the turning point of the psalm? (v. 21b)

When in the experience of Jesus on the cross do you think this happened for Him?

What were the Messiah's responses to God's deliverance? (vv. 22–26)

What would be the response in the world to the Messiah's praise of God? (vv. 27–31)

How are you and all other Christians part of the fulfillment of Psalm 22:27–31?

A MESSIANIC STRAIN IN OTHER SONGS

The Holy Spirit took the poets beyond their own understanding when they prophesied of the Messiah. Sometimes the messianic element is a short part of a psalm that is otherwise not about the Messiah. Let's look at some of them.

Psalm 69:9

David wrote about his devotion to the tabernacle. How did the apostle John apply this text to the ideal Son of David, the Messiah? (John 2:13–17)

Psalm 118:19–29

How did Jesus apply Psalm 118:22, 23 to Himself and those around Him? (Matt. 21:40–46; Mark 12:9–12; Luke 20:15–19)

How did the Holy Spirit move Peter to apply Psalm 118:22 to Jesus and the Jewish rulers? (Acts 4:8–12)

How did Peter broaden his use of Psalm 118:22 when writing to Gentiles and to Jews who had not been involved in Jesus' death? (1 Pet. 2:4–8)

In the New Testament, Psalm 118:26 rang from the lips of multitudes in praise. Why? (Matt. 21:9; Mark 11:9, 10; Luke 19:37–40; John 12:12, 13)

Psalm 41:9

How did Jesus apply David's lament about betrayal by a friend to His situation? (John 13:18, 21–30)

Psalm 69:21

Another seemingly minor detail of a lament of David proved to be a prophecy from God's Spirit. How was it fulfilled in the Messiah's suffering? (Matt. 27:33, 34, 48; Mark 15:22, 23, 36)

Psalm 34:20

This verse is from a psalm of praise by David for deliverance from King Saul. How did it find a prophetic fulfillment in the Messiah? (John 19:31–37; see also Ex. 12:43–46)

Psalm 16:10

"Declared to Be the Son of God with Power" (Ps. 16:10). The apostles clearly recognized this verse as forecasting the resurrection of Jesus. Peter quotes this verse in his sermon on the Day of Pentecost (Acts 2:27), and Paul quotes this verse in his early preaching at Antioch of Pisidia (Acts 13:35).

The sufficiency of Christ's work of atonement is declared in the Resurrection (Rom. 6; 2 Tim. 1:10; Heb. 2:9–18; 1 Pet. 2:18), and by the Resurrection Jesus was "declared to be the Son of God with power" (Rom. 1:4). He has completed the work He came to do and has ascended to the right hand of the Father. Now we look forward in hope, for having broken the power of death, He has introduced the promise of eternal life to all who receive Him as Messiah (John 6:40).[3]

1. *Spirit-Filled Life Bible* (Nashville, TN: Thomas Nelson Publishers, 1991), 772, Chart: "The Christ of Psalms."

2. Ibid., 770–771, "Kingdom Dynamics: 'Establishing' God's Throne."

3. Ibid., 764, "Kingdom Dynamics: Declared to be the Son of God with Power."

Lesson 11/A Song of Repentance

Everyone has heard of *The Scarlet Letter*, but few read it anymore. That's too bad, because *The Scarlet Letter* explores the crucial questions of what sin is and how it is to be handled with God, the community, and self.

The story is set in Puritan New England. The facts are that Hester Prynne committed adultery in her husband's lengthy absence, bore a child, and was sentenced by the community to wear perpetually the letter *A* as an emblem of her sin. The real story involves what goes on in the hearts and spirits of Hester, the Reverend Arthur Dimmesdale who had committed adultery with her but concealed it, and Hester's husband who returned under the name Roger Chillingworth to discover and revenge himself on the adulterer.

Hawthorne's theology was not completely orthodox, but in essence Hester was able to receive forgiveness from God, although not from the townspeople. She was relieved in her heart of her guilt and shame although both were her constant companions in society. The Reverend Dimmesdale was accounted by the church people to be a saint because he seemed so conscious of his unworthiness. The spiritual truth was that he was being consumed by his hypocrisy, shame, and guilt as he preached and ministered to people week after week in his unforgiven state. He knew that his confessions to God were incomplete and insincere as long as he failed to accept publicly the responsibility for his sin.

Roger Chillingworth became a study in the destructive power of revenge and in the spiritual rationale for leaving the righting of wrongs to God alone. Dimmesdale collapsed and died from the debilitating effects of his guilt, but Chillingworth lived on, dead in his soul, killed by the bitterly poisonous idea that anything a wronged person does to get even is right.

Only Hester Prynne walked free and forgiven at the story's end. The *A* on the bosom of her dress meant nothing, because God's forgiveness was in her heart. If Hester had sung a song of repentance it would have been, like the ones in the Psalms, a sadder but wiser song that found an abiding joy in the God who will give us what we never deserve—forgiveness.

A SONG OF GUILT

The seven psalms you will study in this lesson were identified by the early church as penitential psalms to be sung and read during Ash Wednesday services in preparation for the Easter season.[1] Five of them are Davidic psalms, and three of those refer to David's spiritual struggle following his adultery with Bathsheba. Psalm 38 tells of the burden of guilt David bore before he confessed his sin, Psalm 51 records his confession and release from guilt, and Psalm 32 celebrates the blessing of forgiveness. The subject matter of these psalms forms the three divisions of this lesson.

Psalm 38

For what did David pray? (vv. 1, 2) Was he asking to escape all consequences for his sin?

What were the physical and emotional symptoms of David's distress caused by his sin? (vv. 3–10)

PHYSICAL   EMOTIONAL

What were the responses of some of those around David to his distress caused by sin? (vv. 11, 12)

What was David's distressed response to his opponents? (vv. 13, 14)

What was David's hope in the midst of his distress over his sins? (vv. 15, 16)

How did David summarize the situation facing him as he talked to the Lord? (vv. 17–22)

Psalms 6 and 102

You have already studied Psalms 6 and 102 as songs of sorrow in Lesson 4. The sorrow of these poems springs from a heavy load of unconfessed sin. Notice the similarity of Psalm 6:1 and Psalm 38:1.

Why is a person burdened with unconfessed sin liable to develop physical ailments or symptoms?

What is there about the anguish of guilt that makes a person think about dying?

Why is a guilty person often unable to sleep?

Why does preoccupation with guilt make a person conscious of and vulnerable to his enemies?

A SONG OF CONFESSION

David was not able to confess and release to God his sin of adultery with Bathsheba during the period of time when he was trying to cover it up (2 Sam. 11:6–27). After God sent Nathan the prophet to David to expose his sin (2 Sam. 12:1–15), David was freed to cast his crushing burden of guilt on the Lord.

Psalm 51

What did David want from God, and on what basis did he ask it? (vv. 1, 2)

What facts did David admit in his confession? (vv. 3–6)

What things did David ask for as steps in the restoration of his sin-broken relationship with God? (vv. 7–11)

What had happened to King Saul, David's predecessor, when God removed His Spirit from him? (1 Sam. 16:14–23)

What things did David promise the Lord in response to forgiveness of sin? (vv. 12–17)

The Law did not provide for a sacrifice for David's intentional sin. What was the only meaningful sacrifice he could offer God? (vv. 16, 17)

When his confession was completed, what sort of prayer was David able to offer God? (vv. 18, 19)

Psalm 143

This psalm of David reinforces the confident expectation of forgiveness expressed in Psalm 51. It also looks to the Holy Spirit as the enabler of a life of renewed service.

What doctrinal point about sin did David remind the Lord of in verse 2?

What request did he base on that doctrinal truth?

David was referring to his human enemy in verses 3 and 4, but spiritual enemies function the same way. How does Satan act like this in the life of a Christian?

What value does remembering former days of pleasant spiritual fellowship with God have in times of repentance and confession? (vv. 5, 6)

Psalm 143 ends with a collection of prayers that may be based on David's remembrance of better days in his walk with the Lord. What things did David ask of God? (vv. 7–12)

v. 7

v. 8

v. 9

v. 10

v. 11

v. 12

What is the relationship between the sinner's spirit (v. 7) and God's Spirit? (v. 10)

A SONG OF FORGIVENESS

After David confessed his sin of adultery with Bathsheba and the subsequent complicity in the death of her husband (2 Sam. 11:14–17), he experienced a sense of forgiveness that was positively euphoric compared to the depressing misery of his period of guilt and shame.

Psalm 32

What did David describe as a blessing from God on a man? (vv. 1, 2)

What conclusion did Paul draw from this passage in his epistle to the Romans? (Rom. 4:5–8)

   WORD WEALTH

There are three important terms in Psalm 32:1 and 2 which express how God deals graciously with the sins of a repentant believer. The first word, translated "to forgive," is *nasa'*. Its sense is "to take up and carry away." Sins thus forgiven are removed from God's consideration. The second word, translated "to cover," is *casah,* which means "to conceal" or "to hide." When David stopped hiding his sin (Ps. 32:5) and confessed it, then God hid it in His forgiveness.

The third word, translated "to impute," is *hashab*. To impute means to make a judgment that something—in this case sin—should be accredited to someone. In Psalm 32 sins are *not* imputed. A person is blessed when his sins are not charged to his account.

In contrast to the blessedness of a person whose sins are forgiven, what is the condition of a person with unconfessed sins? (vv. 3, 4)

How is forgiveness a form of God's protection? (vv. 6, 7)

What advice does the Lord give directly about confession and forgiveness? Why is His animal comparison so apt? (vv. 8, 9)

What does the forgiven man have to shout about? (vv. 10, 11)

Psalm 130

This seventh penitential psalm is another of the songs of sorrow studied in Lesson 4. There you contemplated the inner turmoil of the psalmist who had felt like he was drowning in a sea of iniquity. The overall tone of Psalm 130, however, is not despair. The mood is anticipated by the watch for the sunrise in verses 5 and 6 and declared in verses 7 and 8.

Each line of verse 7 contains a step away from the despair of sin. What are the steps and what do they mean?

STEP   MEANING

WORD WEALTH

"Redemption" translates the Hebrew noun *pedut*. The idea of ransom exists in the family of words to which *pedut* belongs. There is always a price to be paid for sin to achieve forgiveness. It is part of God's mercy that He has provided the payment.

FAITH ALIVE

Have you ever had an encounter with real guilt as a result of sinful thoughts or behavior (not the false kind produced by perfectionism) that caused you emotional or physical distress? If so, describe it here, not to share with anyone, but to explore its meaning for your spiritual life.

How did you eventually come to realize that you had to confess that sin, and how did you confess it privately and/or publicly?

As you have thought about this situation, are there any parts of your sin that you have never confessed or that are still hidden but should be revealed? (Confession should be no more public than the offense.)

If something about this sin should be confessed further, how could you do it?

What act of confession of sin brought you the most joy in the Lord? Was it at your time of salvation or was it a subsequent occasion that was a high point in your spiritual life? Describe your joy of confession.

The Holy Spirit indwells Christians, but what does our sin do to our relationship with Him? (Eph. 4:30; 1 Thess. 5:19)

What spiritual truths can you share with more understanding because you have experienced God's gracious forgiveness of sins through the course of your Christian life?

1. Willem A. VanGemeren, "Psalms," *The Expositor's Bible*, Vol. 5 (Grand Rapids, MI: Zondervan Publishing House, 1991), 96.

Lesson 12/A Song of Salvation

On March 30, 1991, Emily Davis Mobley and fifty-five other cave enthusiasts entered Lechugilla Cave in Carlsbad Caverns National Park on a mapping expedition. Lechugilla had been discovered in 1986 and already fifty-five miles of passages reaching a depth of more than 1,500 feet had been charted under strict supervision by the National Park Service. Only spelunkers like twenty-two-year veteran Emily could gain access to the cave.

On Sunday Emily was charting the depth of a pit miles from the entrance and a thousand feet below the surface when a boulder broke loose from the side of the pit and crushed her left leg. Between Emily and the outside world was a steep, rugged ascent barred by cliffs of more than a hundred feet and by stretches of passageway so small that explorers have to wriggle through on their stomachs. Emily couldn't go anywhere.

Emergency preparedness is part of every good caving expedition, so a rescue was underway as the dust settled. A doctor on the expedition immobilized the shattered leg and strapped Emily to a stretcher. Emily's friends gathered from around the United States to form shifts of rescuers that changed every few hours to carry, drag, and hoist her back to safety.

She dangled vertically from ropes with her weight pressing down on her shattered leg. She was "turtled" through low passages, passed along the backs of a line of rescuers down on hands and knees. She was jostled over acres of large boulders.

Before dawn on Thursday, ninety-six hours into the rescue, the team told Emily that they were approaching the cave mouth. The danger was over. Through the pain of her injury and the frustration of being immobilized for four days, she began to sing "Are the Stars Out Tonight?"

The stars were out to greet Emily in the early desert morn. Later the doctors at the Guadelupe Medical Center in Carlsbad, New Mexico, put a bolt into her upper shin. Emily Davis Mobley was back from the depths.

When the psalmists cried out to God for deliverance, they, too, cried out from the depths of danger, despair, or guilt. They believed that the salvation God gave in response to their pleas was no less spectacular than Emily's seems to us.

SONG OF DANGER

Among the psalms you will study that celebrate the deliverance God provides are two that focus on the need for salvation. The psalmists might appeal to the Lord because of physical danger posed by enemies or sickness or because of spiritual danger posed by sin.

Psalm 69

What do the images of verses 1–3 express about the troubles David was facing?

IMAGE   MEANING

Water up to the neck

Deep mire

Floods

Dry throat

Failed eyes

What did the floods and mire represent? (v. 4)

What did David pray for besides his deliverance from enemies?

v. 5

v. 6

What spiritual activities were David's enemies mocking him about? (vv. 7–12)

How would David's sins (v. 5) have exposed him and others to mockery? (vv. 6–12)

How did David expand his opening prayer for deliverance? (vv. 13–21)

What did David pray with regard to his enemies who were mocking God? (vv. 22–28)

 BEHIND THE SCENES

Seventeen of the Psalms contain prayers that express hatred toward and ask for God's judgment on the psalmists' enemies. These are called Imprecatory Psalms, because *imprecation* is the fancy word for "prayers of revenge."

The psalmists wrote these prayers under the inspiration of the Holy Spirit. Their spiritual insights were aligned with God's so well at the time that their prayers express God's righteous hatred of sin rather than the private all-too-fallible vendettas of the psalmists.

We can learn from these Imprecatory Psalms that God hates evil and deals with evildoers. We can even learn that He will listen to us when we express our anger and frustration with people we don't like, but He will always point us back to Jesus' command to love our neighbors (Matt. 5:43–48).

What did David vow to the Lord in response to salvation? (vv. 29–33)

To whom did David appeal that they might praise the Lord for His salvation? (vv. 34–36)

Psalm 71

This anonymous psalm is a song of the dangers of advanced age. Even the believer who has trusted the Lord from his childhood faces unique problems in later years.

What is the elderly psalmist's confidence? (vv. 1–3)

Why did the elderly psalmist have confidence about praying for deliverance? (vv. 4–6)

What was the psalmist afraid of? (vv. 7, 9–13)

What did the psalmist want instead of his fears? (vv. 8, 14–18)

What advantage did the age of the psalmist give him in facing his dangers of aging? (vv. 19–21)

What did the elderly psalmist promise the Lord? (vv. 22–24)

FAITH ALIVE

How can you become more aware of the faith lessons you can learn from the elderly saints in your church?

How could your church give elderly saints more opportunity to express what the Lord has done for them so younger adults can benefit from their wisdom?

How could you encourage the faith of an older saint who may be struggling with the limitations of aging?

Whom might you encourage in this way?

When could you offer this encouragement?

SONG OF CONFIDENCE

The next two songs of salvation express trust in the Lord to deliver from the kinds of danger lamented about in the previous section of this lesson.

Psalm 17

How did David describe his prayer? (v. 1)

Why did David expect the Lord to vindicate him? (vv. 2–5)

Since it is clear from other psalms that David committed serious sins, how can he, or any other sinner, make the claims of verses 2–5?

In David's prayer for protection (vv. 6–9), how do the two images in verse 8 establish his confidence about the Lord's answer?

To what did David liken his enemies, and how did they fit the description? (vv. 10–12)

What contrasting fates did David desire for his enemies and himself? (vv. 13, 15)

BIBLE EXTRA

Psalm 17:14 is difficult to translate and to interpret. Some assume the Hebrew text has been confused in transmission through the centuries and make slight adjustments so verse 14 refers to the righteous rather than the wicked. If the text is correct, David was reminding his readers that the wicked, even when under judgment, may prosper materially, pass on their ill-gotten gains to their children, and be pleased with themselves.

This smug self-assurance is part of God's judgment. Any wealthy person who is certain he or she is self-sufficient and secure in their family succession are deluded and foolish.They are one disaster away from annihilation but cannot see it.[1] See Psalm 49 for a full discussion of this issue by the sons of Korah.

Psalm 85

This song of salvation followed a time of captivity (v. 1). Probably a descendant of Korah wrote this after the Babylonian captivity when the survivors of the Exile looked to the Lord to restore Jerusalem and Judah to political prominence. This psalmist knew there was only one power to trust for a restored nation.

What things had the Lord done recently that gave the psalmist confidence to pray to Him? (vv. 1–3)

Based on the Lord's recent blessing, what did the psalmist ask for right then? (vv. 4–7)

What answers to his prayers did the psalmist confidently expect? (vv. 8, 9)

What is there about God's character that guarantees ultimate vindication of God's people? (v. 10)

What do God's people always have to look forward to as a basis for hope? (vv. 11–13)

SONG OF VICTORY

These two psalms celebrate God's salvation that was pleaded for in the songs of danger and anticipated in the songs of confidence. The salvation dealt with in these psalms is deliverance from physical danger, but Psalms 34 and 118 contain messianic predictions that connect God's physical salvation with His salvation from sin. God is a Savior from all the threats facing people.

Psalm 34

Psalm 34 is the most exuberant of the psalms David wrote during his time of persecution and pursuit by King Saul (see BEHIND THE SCENES, Lesson 6, p. 78). It is another alphabetical psalm (see BEHIND THE SCENES, Lesson 1, p. 19).

How did David elaborate on his invitation to "bless the LORD at all times"? (vv. 1–3)

What did David testify happens when the needy cry out to the Lord for deliverance? (vv. 4–7)

In verses 8–14, what ideas did David include as parts of the fear of the Lord?

Why can the righteous cry out for salvation with confidence? (vv. 15–17)

What is it about the righteous that the Lord responds to? (vv. 18–22)

Psalm 118

This anonymous song of salvation has been used historically in Jewish worship during the Passover Seder and the service for the Feast of Tabernacles.[2]

For what abundantly clear reason did the psalmist call on his readers to give thanks to the Lord? (vv. 1–4, 29)

What effect does the psalmist achieve by the repetition of calls to Israel, the house of Aaron, and all who fear the Lord to give thanks? (vv. 2–4)

What were the results of the Lord's salvation of the psalmist? (vv. 5–7)

What conclusion did the psalmist reach because of the Lord's salvation? (vv. 8, 9)

What happened to those who attacked the psalmist? (vv. 10–14)

Verses 15–29 conclude Psalm 118 with a hymn of praise for the salvation of the Lord. What do you think each of the following images contributes to the psalmist's description of the Lord's salvation?

The right hand of the Lord (vv. 15, 16)

Gates (vv. 19, 20)

The stone (v. 22)

Light (v. 27)

The sacrifice bound to the altar (v. 27)

FAITH ALIVE

When and how has the Lord delivered you from dangers to your physical life?

What present and eternal dangers were you in when you cried out to the Lord for salvation from your sins?

What events and scriptural promises have given you certainty that the Lord can be trusted for daily deliverance and eternal salvation?

Choose one verse from Psalm 34 or 118 that best captures your attitudes toward the Lord as your Savior and write it here as an expression of praise.

1. Franz Delitzsch, *Biblical Commentary on Psalms,* Vol. I (Grand Rapids, MI: William B. Eerdmans Publishing Company, 1968), 242, 243.

2. Willem A. VanGemeren, "Psalms," *The Expositor's Bible,* Vol. 5 (Grand Rapids, MI: Zondervan Publishing House, 1991), 96.

Lesson 13/A Song of Witness

Regardless of a person's opinion of the individual, one of the interesting features of Ross Perot's quixotic candidacy for the presidency of the United States in 1992 was his use of testimonials in his lengthy info-mercials. Rather than having general statements about his character and qualifications for office, Mr. Perot had people tell their stories of what he had done for them.

The wife of a Viet Nam War POW told how government officials gave her the runaround before deciding that nothing could be done. A telephone call to Ross Perot reportedly triggered a flurry of activity by the Texas businessman that resulted in the release of some prisoners, including the narrator's husband. The former POW joined his wife at that point and recounted how the treatment at the hand of his captors improved at the time Mr. Perot began to intervene.

A small businessman told how local authorities wouldn't repair a flood-damaged roadway in time to prevent area businesses from failing. He claimed that another telephone call set to work the problem-solving skills of Ross Perot. Red tape was eliminated by bypassing bureaucrats, and within a month the road was open again.

A third person told of a son injured in an accident. The necessary medical equipment to save his life wasn't available. Enter Ross Perot and his helicopters, and the young man was saved, and Mr. Perot even attended the young man's subsequent wedding.

A personal witness is a powerful, persuasive tool. That's why this politician chose to use it in his campaign, just as others have. A personal witness is a way of addressing the heart as well as the head. That's why the Lord inspired the psalmists to bear witness to His faithfulness to them individually and to His people as a nation. That's why Christians still need to bear witness of what God has done for them. The heart often must lead the head to God.

A WITNESS TO GOD'S CHARACTER

The first three songs of witness in this lesson are psalms of David that rejoice in the qualities God exhibits in His gracious dealings with His children.

Psalm 63

This psalm was written when David was king (v. 11) and when he was away from the sanctuary of the Lord (v. 2). According to the superscription of the psalm, David was "in the wilderness of Judah," which may refer to the time when he was forced out of Jerusalem by the rebellion of his son Absalom (2 Sam. 15:13–17). In spite of these circumstances, David testified to the greatness of the Lord.

When did David find himself meditating on the character of God? (vv. 1, 6)

How did David describe his longing for God? (vv. 1, 7, 8)

What qualities of God's character satisfied David's meditations when he was in exile from the sanctuary? (vv. 2, 3, 7, 8, 11)

When David reflected on God's character, what did he realize about his enemies? (vv. 9, 10)

Psalm 103

This hymn of praise is one of David's greatest songs of witness to the mercy of God.

Whom did David call on to bless the Lord? (vv. 1, 2, 20–22)

What did David want his soul to remember about the Lord? (vv. 2–5)

BEHIND THE SCENES

God's Saving and Healing Benefit (Ps. 103:3). This is a definite Old Testament promise of bodily healing based upon the character of Yahweh as the Healer. It is clear that the dimension of healing promised here is specifically to include physical wholeness. The text reinforces the healing covenant, since the Hebrew word for "diseases" is from the same root as the word for disease in Exodus 15:26 where the Lord promised to heal His people who obey Him. Further the word for "to heal" is the same in both passages, with the idea of mending or curing.

These two passages bear from the Old Testament that the Lord not only forgives iniquities; He heals our diseases. If under the former covenant bodily healing was pointedly included with the Father's many other benefits, we can rejoice and rest in faith. The New Covenant "glory" exceeds everything of the Old, and we can be certain that God, in Christ, has made a complete provision for the well-being of our total person.[1]

How does the Lord show His mercy to His people? (vv. 6–14)

How great is the Lord's mercy? (vv. 11–14)

To whom does the Lord show mercy? (vv. 17, 18)

Why do people need God's mercy so badly? (vv. 13–16)

Psalm 145

This is the last of David's alphabetical psalms (see BEHIND THE SCENES, Lesson 1, page 19). God's attributes and actions are the themes of David's song of witness. Underline in your Bible all the occurrences in Psalm 145 of words of worship, such as "extol," "bless," "praise," "declare," "meditate," "speak of," "utter," "talk of," and "make known." How much of the psalm consists of a promise to witness about the Lord?

What about the Lord did David desire to extol in the following verses?

v. 2

v. 3

v. 4

v. 5

v. 6

v. 7

v. 8

v. 9

v. 10

v. 11

v. 12

v. 13

How does the Lord respond to the needy who call on His name? (vv. 14–20)

A WITNESS BY MY LIFE

These two psalms recount present, personal experiences of the psalmist or the people. They witness of the daily loving-kindness of the Lord.

Psalm 124

This song of witness by David is an expression by the nation of Israel of how the Lord had delivered them from the vicious attack of an enemy people. For centuries after David wrote it, pilgrims on their way to Jerusalem to participate in the major religious festivals sang this psalm as preparation for worship.

What would have happened to Israel if the Lord had not been on their side? (vv. 1–5)

What are the images of defeat David used in his poem, and what aspect of suffering does each image convey? (vv. 3–7)

How does the image of the broken snare and escaped bird help prepare the reader to agree with the statements of praise in verses 6 and 8?

Psalm 139

This song of witness is the most intensely personal of David's psalms. In it David revealed how he thought about God, how he trusted God to care for him, and how he prayed to God in private.

What did the searching omniscience (all-knowingness) of God know about David? (vv. 2–4)

What benefit did David receive based on God's omniscient search of his life? (v. 5)

What conclusion had David reached because of God's omnipresence (His everywhereness)? (vv. 7, 8)

What benefits did David understand to be his because of God's omnipresence? (vv. 9–12)

How did David understand the Lord to have been involved in his life before his birth? (vv. 13–16)

How did David value his night-and-day thoughts about God? (vv. 17, 18)

In contrast to his thoughts about God (vv. 17, 18), what were David's thoughts about godless people? (vv. 19–22)

What did David want to result from his time spent enjoying the Lord's greatness and goodness? (vv. 23, 24)

A WITNESS FROM HISTORY

The two songs of witness in this section record aspects of the history of Israel which the nation looked to as reminders of God's righteousness and mercy. You will look at them in the order of their historical subject matter rather than the numerical sequence of the psalms.

Psalm 105

This song of witness testifies to the establishment of God's covenant with the nation of Israel. Although the psalm is anonymous, the first fifteen verses are attributed to David at the time he had the ark of the covenant brought to Jerusalem (1 Chr. 16:8–22).

What did the psalmist call on Israel to do in the first five verses?

By what two ancestral labels did the psalmist identify Israel? (v. 6)

In your Bible underline all the references to Abraham and Jacob in Psalm 105. Then circle all occurrences of the words "covenant," "oath," and "inheritance." What aspect of the covenant history is noted in verses 9–12?

What aspect of the covenant history is noted in verses 42–45?

Psalm 105:16–22 summarizes the events of Genesis 37—41. What were they?

Psalm 105:23–25 summarizes the events from Genesis 42—Exodus 1. What happened?

Psalm 105:26–36 summarizes the events of Exodus 2:1—12:30. What were they?

Psalm 105:37–41 summarizes the events of Exodus 12:31—17:7. What happened?

Verse 8 summarizes the Lord's activity testified to in this song of witness. Copy it in the space provided.

Psalm 68

This song of witness by David testified to the Lord's activity in Israel's history from the Exodus to the time of David and then looked to the future when the Lord will reign over all the earth.

What actions did David call on the Lord to take in verses 1, 2?

What are the righteous to do in anticipation of these actions? (vv. 3, 4)

 FAITH ALIVE

YAH (Ps. 68:4) is a shortened poetic form of *Yahweh,* the name for God which usually appears in English as "Jehovah." The Hebrews would not pronounce *Yahweh.* They regarded the name as too holy for human lips, so they said "my Lord," *'adonai,* whenever they came across *Yahweh* in the Scripture.

Through the centuries, the Jews began to write the vowels of *'adonai* under the consonants of *Yahweh* as a shorthand reminder to say *'adonai.* The first Christian scholars to study Hebrew in the Middle Ages didn't know this, so they pronounced the consonants from one name with the vowels of the other and came up with Jehovah.

YAH survives in English as the final syllable of the praise exclamation "hallelujah!" This is the Hebrew command "Praise YAH" or "Praise the LORD."

What is there about the character of God that has caused Him to act on behalf of His people? (vv. 5, 6, 19, 20)

What was YAH like when He led Israel out of Egypt and through the desert? (vv. 7–10)

What was YAH like when He led Israel in conquering the Promised Land? (vv. 11–14)

YAH chose Jerusalem, or Zion, as His mountain. For what purposes did He choose His mountain? (vv. 15–18, 21–23)

What was the procession like when David brought the ark of God to Jerusalem? (vv. 24–27)

What did David expect to happen in the future when the Lord's reign will extend over all the earth? (vv. 28–31)

What did David invite the kingdoms of the earth to sing as a witness about the Lord? (vv. 32–35)

 FAITH ALIVE

As you reflect back through this study of the Psalms, what attributes of God has the Spirit of God impressed on you as subjects you should talk about in your witness for Him?

What is the Lord doing in your life now that should become part of your witness for Him?

What has the Lord done in the past for you, for your family, and for your church that can be part of your witness to the character and faithfulness of God?

Use Psalm 124 as a model and write a brief psalm of testimony about God's faithfulness to you.

What has been the most important spiritual insight God has shown you from His Word during this study of the Psalms?

What patterns of worship and praise can you adopt from the Psalms in your private and public worship to enrich your fellowship with the Lord?

1. *Spirit-Filled Life Bible* (Nashville, TN: Thomas Nelson Publishers, 1991), 841, "Kingdom Dynamics: God's Saving and Healing Benefit."